DISCOVERING
THE THAMES

*A motorist's guide to the best view points
and the most interesting features.*

Leon Metcalfe

Shire Publications Ltd

CONTENTS

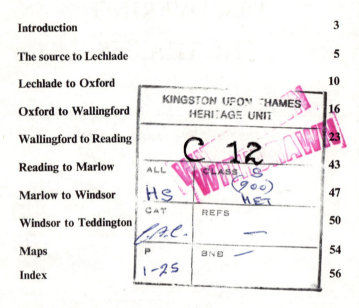

Photographs and cover illustration by Derek Pratt. Line drawings by Edward Stamp.

Copyright ©1981 by Leon Metcalfe. First published 1969. Second edition 1981. No. 47 in the 'Discovering' series. ISBN 0 85263 566 4.

INTRODUCTION

The river Thames is something of an enigma; it does not appear to begin where the experts say it does, in fact the experts are divided even on this point. Some say the source is at Seven Springs near Cheltenham, while the majority have decided that the Thames begins at Trewsbury Mead near Cirencester. Where does the Thames end? Some consider Teddington sees the end of the Thames and the beginning of London River; perhaps the end is in the estuary or somewhere out to sea. When did the river first flow in its present valley? Did it ever flow from Wales to the Rhine, as some suggest? These and many more unanswered riddles come to mind when one thinks about the Thames rather than accepting it as it is. Why, even the river's name is in doubt; is it Isis or Thames? Perhaps the very fact that the Thames is an enigma is one of its important attractions.

This book, however, is devoted to seeking out and enjoying the more tangible attractions which the river has to offer. We want to know its history and what changes there have been over the centuries, what scenic pleasures it has to offer, what effect man has had on it and, perhaps most important of all, how to get to see all these facets of the river Thames.

The Thames rises in the foothills of the Cotswolds and flows eastwards towards Oxford, searching it seems for a gap in the chalk hills to the south. At Oxford it turns south having found the gap between the Berkshire Downs and the Chilterns. At this stage it has grown so wide it appears almost to fill the gap and to leave no room for those twin villages of Streatley and Goring. At Reading, with the help of the river Kennet, it decides to investigate the slopes of the Chilterns. At Marlow the river becomes bored with the chalk and flows south east through Eton and Windsor, but at Weybridge it is the sea that urges it to flow eastward again through London, and on to lose itself beyond the estuary.

This waterway flowing almost completely across England has for centuries been used by Man as a route for the transportation of men and materials. In more recent times, efforts of varying degree and success have been made to improve this route, and for these endeavours we must be thankful, for without them the Thames would still be a battle-ground—a constant source of grumbles and complaints between landowners, millers, weir and flash-lock keepers, bargemen and riverside dwellers. Each, at one time, struggled for personal gain or profit against the rest. The first properly organized body for navigation improvements on the Thames was the Oxford/Burcot Commission of 1605, but this only had local effect, and it was to be a wait of about 150 years before the Thames throughout its length was considered, and a further century before an almost complete locking system had evolved on the length of the river. With the Thames Conservancy Act of 1857 we have the first appearance of the Thames Conservancy, the present controlling authority. Their job is wide-ranging indeed; they are responsible for the river from just below Teddington Locks up to the source, the drainage of the area, the prevention of pollution, the supply of water to towns and cities, especially London, and above all the navigation on the river.

On 1st April 1974 the newly legislated Thames Water Authority became responsible for all aspects of water supply and usage related to the river and as a consequence the Thames Conservancy is now only a division of the Authority.

When the canal era was in full swing in this country it was natural that the canal engineers would look with envy at the natural waterway of the river Thames. James Brindley once said that rivers existed only to supply water to canals! It was he who began the Oxford Canal joining the Thames to the midland canal system. The rivers Thames and Severn were connected by a canal and the Avon was joined to the Kennet, the latter being a tributary of the Thames; two routes to the West country and one to the Midlands. Yet another canal to join the Thames was the Wilts./Berks. from Abingdon-on-Thames to Semington on the Kennet and Avon Canal. Of these four 'man-made rivers' two have vanished, one is struggling to get water back into its channel, leaving only Brindley's Oxford Canal still functioning. In one respect the river has died also, in that little in the way of goods is carried now. Today is the day of the pleasure boat, and no longer the scene of feuds and floods.

In this introduction I have tried to give a general topographical picture of the whole river, and also some indication of the development of the Thames as a good, reliable waterway. The rest of the book will, I hope, complete to some extent the history the river has seen and the areas most likely to provide pleasure from the scenic point of view.

THE SOURCE TO LECHLADE

1. Source of the river Thames

Leave Cirencester on the A429 towards Malmesbury. This is the old Roman Road of Fosse Way. In 1¾ miles the A429 forks left. Continue straight on for a further 1½ miles on the A433, Tetbury Road. Just before the railway bridge comes into view and by a group of cottages, Thames Head Bridge is negotiated. This bridge carries the road over the long disused Thames/Severn Canal. Immediately beyond this are the culverts allowing the infant Thames to pass under the road. Proceed beyond this point along the road up towards the railway bridge. On the left before the bridge is a lay-by. Park here.

To reach the spring named as the source of the Thames walk back along the road for approximately 100 yards when, on the left, a track down to a field gate will be reached. After passing through the gate one can find the culverts mentioned earlier. These are situated 50 yards to the right under the road. So shaded and overgrown are they that it is quite possible that water may be found in them. I mention this because it is unlikely that water, especially Thames water, will be seen anywhere else on this walk. Looking across the field from this point, it is usually possible to mark the line of the river by noticing the tree-line and other vegetation curving its way towards a stone wall near a gate. Cross the field and pass through the gate, and again follow the line of richer vegetation towards a spinney, across another track, to the plaque marking the source of the Thames. The source itself is in fact the usually dry, shallow hollow lined with limestone.

This is Trewsbury Mead, and behind the plaque is an old encampment called Trewsbury castle, with its double ditch. Running back towards the main road among the trees the course of the disused Thames/Severn Canal can be investigated.

If it is imperative that the true Thames water be seen then cross back over the main road and follow the line of the stream bed again for perhaps a ¼ of a mile or more, depending on the recent rainfall, until the river, or The Brook as it is called locally, is discovered.

2. Viaduct—north east of Kemble

From the lay-by drive back 1½ miles towards Cirencester until the A429 Malmesbury road is reached. Turn right on to this road and drive for nearly 2 miles to a point where the road passes between the remains of railway embankments. Parking is available on both sides of the road. (Three-quarters of a mile before this, between a righthand and then a lefthand junction, the disused

Thames/Severn Canal is crossed again.)

Park near the embankment and the parapets of a bridge, to right and left, will be apparent. This is the first road bridge crossing the river, having running Thames water under it at all times of the year. (Thames Head bridge, the first over the Thames, invariably passes over a dry bed, or perhaps a stagnant pool.) This then, in the true sense of the word, is the motorist's first view of the Thames. It is a pretty spot with walks in both directions alongside the clear, rippling stream-water of the infant Thames.

3. Ewen—The Wild Duck Inn

From the embankment continue along the A429 into Kemble taking the first turning on the left in the village, and in a short distance left again. Towards the edge of this Cotswold village take the left turn signposted to Ewen, just under a mile away.

Half a mile from the last junction the river is crossed on its journey round the south side of the village. In this area the Thames does not confine itself to one stream but many, and it is often difficult to decide which one is the main stream.

It is interesting to note that the village of Ewen takes its name from the Old English word meaning spring or source of a stream, and on an eighteenth century map made by Isaac Taylor it is spelt 'Yeoing'. On passing through the village one feature which one should not miss is the Wild Duck Inn. Its initial attraction is its setting commanding the junction of the roads. A closer inspection will reveal above and to the right of the door a clock set in a large frame and surrounded by pictures of wild ducks in flight. At the entrance is a ship's binnacle with an inscription. At this inn one Cornelius Uzzle, a hungry extrovert, consumed twelve pounds of bacon, some of it raw, before a gathering of the locals, from whom he extracted money after the display. Perhaps it was not insignificant that it was bacon with which he was stuffing himself!

4. Ashton Keynes—a street of bridges

Turn right beside the Wild Duck Inn and then left in a short distance to take the road towards Somerford Keynes. A mile along this road a lane leads off to the right down to a private dwelling which was once the first mill on the river Thames. It is now called Upper Mill Farm, but the wheel was demolished towards the end of the nineteenth century. Half a mile beyond the mill at the road junction turn right and drive through the village of Somerford Keynes. The Thames flows, as two main streams, a little to the west of the village and, as at least part of the name suggests, the village was once noted as a place where the river could be forded in summer. The Keynes part of the name, as will also be noted for Ashton Keynes, dates from the early thirteenth century when this area was owned by a Norman by the name William de Kaines.

Turn left in the village and follow the Ashton Keynes signs for about one and three quarters of a mile beside the sand and gravel pits. The main village street is notable for its Cotswold stone houses and the little individual bridges crossing the Thames to each house. Although no evidence remains, it is thought that this village was once a busy town depending for its affluence on the river, nowadays only a few feet wide. It was also the site of a monastery—the first of many to be encountered on the banks of the Thames—but again nothing remains.

5. Waterhay bridge and Cricklade

Turn left in Ashton Keynes on the Happylands Road, to Cricklade, and after a mile Waterhay bridge is crossed. This was built to replace an earlier bridge in 1895 and crosses the Swillbrook just before this stream joins up with the Thames, to the left of the bridge. After crossing the Swillbrook fork left and travel for 1½ miles till reaching the B4040. Turn left here for Cricklade. This is an old market town, the first on the Thames, but some of its charm is lost in the rumble of the trucks and lorries as they pass through the town on the A419 trunk road to Cirencester and on to Gloucester. The Romans built this road, the Irmin Street, but not through Cricklade. They were content to by-pass the town by making use of the ancient ford half a mile east of the town bridge. On each side of Cricklade town bridge is mounted a plaque bearing the inscription: *Rebuilt by the Feoffees of the Cricklade Waylands AD 1854*. The 'feoffees' was the name given to the estate trustees, and money raised from the Waylands estate is still used to help reduce the local rate in the town.

To find a river walk follow Abingdon Court Lane and turn left down a short 'no through road' to a farmyard, and in the corner on the right is a stile and public footpath along by the river in the direction of the ford.

Thoughts of serious navigation of the river come to mind at Cricklade, the spelling of which was originally Criccagelad, meaning 'the place with wharves where the river may be crossed'. Alfred crossed the river here to do battle with the Danes who later plundered the town in 1015.

6. Kempsford—church and house

Leave Cricklade on the A419 towards Cirencester and join the dual carriageway. Almost immediately indicate right and cross to the opposite carriageway to head for Kempsford, which requires taking the first turning on the left. Three miles along this road, a little way past a turning on the left to Marston Meysey, a farm track will be seen running beside a new barn. Follow this track, which is rather rough in places, down to a round house and a typical humpbacked canal bridge. Here once again we have evidence of the old Thames/Severn Canal. The round houses were a unique feature of this canal and though this one is in a poor state it is well worth a visit to observe its design and construction. Returning to the road turn right and continue the journey to Kempsford. A mile further along the road in the middle of a field on the right is yet another canal bridge, rising from nothing, passing over nothing, and descending again on the far side.

At the far end of the village of Kempsford the road turns sharply to the left, but to find the Thames drive straight on towards the church which is on the right. The tower rising from the church was built by John of Gaunt as a memorial to his first wife Blanche. He was married twice more, the last time to Catherine Swynford, one of his mistresses, and it was one of their sons, Bolingbroke, who later became Henry IV.

The river can be seen here by obtaining the permission of the owner of the house. This is situated beyond the church past the beautiful stone barns which may once have belonged to John of Gaunt's estate, as his house was near the site of the present dwelling. This earlier house was the scene of an unfortunate murder. Lady Maud, sister-in-law of John, was harbouring one of her brothers-in-law from his enemies when her husband returned and, seeing them together on the poorly-lit terrace overlooking the river, jumped to the wrong conclusions. He forced the man, his brother, away and pushed his wife to her death in the Thames. Later when he discovered his error he fled, stricken with remorse. Lady Maud, of course, now walks the waters of the Thames in ghostly form!

7. Lechlade

From the church at Kempsford turn back through the village and take the right fork. On the edge of the village turn right for Whelford a mile and a half away. Continue straight through Whelford and across the river Coln, a tributary of the Thames, and turn right at the main road a mile ahead. This road is the A417 Cirencester to Lechlade road. In Lechlade turn right on the A361 Swindon road and cross the river Thames. Beyond the bridge on the right is a large riverside field given over to free

Lechlade

car parking. From this situation the town, river, towpath and bridge can all be explored without having to walk too far.

The town takes its name from the small tributary of the Thames the Leach, or Lech, which joins the river to the south east of the town. To reach the town walk along the towpath towards the bridge, past what once were wharves which would be lined with barges loaded with a wide variety of goods ranging from building materials to cheese. Lechlade was the last Thames town before the barges joined the Thames/Severn Canal west of the town. The warves are now lined with pleasure boats for hire. The bridge, now supplied with traffic lights because it is so narrow, was built by the people of the town in 1792 to replace a ferry. It was, of course, a toll bridge and, as the toll was a halfpenny,

9

then it follows that the bridge was called Halfpenny bridge. The toll house still stands on the town side of the bridge. In the town the 600 years old inn with the misnomer New Inn is said to have been a retreat for Dick Turpin, who hid in the cellars while he was being sought by the Bow Street Runners. Another famous guest at this old coaching inn was Shelley, the poet.

8. Inglesham church

From the car park at Lechlade turn right on to the A361 Swindon road and drive three-quarters of a mile. At this point there is a turning on the right down a lane leading to Inglesham church; it is not signposted but the turning occurs immediately after the 'Inglesham' village sign. Parking is available outside this riverside church before reaching the farm.

This twelfth century church was once a priory chapel, the priory itself being the farmhouse nearby. The church was presented to the abbot of Beaulieu by King John and although it was restored at the end of the nineteenth century by William Morris, who enjoyed its peace and solitude, it still retains all its old character. The soft darkness inside this little church, (the chancel is not much more than 20 feet long), enhances the interior fittings and furniture.

LECHLADE TO OXFORD

9. St. John's lock and bridge

Leave Lechlade on the A417 towards Faringdon, and in three-quarters of a mile the river will be reached at St. John's bridge. Parking is available before reaching the bridge or, after crossing the bridge, on the right.

Access to the lock is from the south end of the bridge on the upstream side. From this point a good view is had of Halfpenny bridge and the town of Lechlade half a mile upstream. The lock was built in 1789 as a result of the building of the canal upstream of Lechlade, and it is the first lock on the river. The original lock cottage was built in 1830 on the far bank but was transferred to its present site in 1905. The Victorian statue of Father Thames, originally from Crystal Palace, was moved here from Trewsbury Mead in 1974.

The earliest reported bridge at this point was a wooden one but at the beginning of the thirteenth century it was replaced by one made of stone. After much alteration and repair this old bridge was eventually pulled down in 1884 and the present bridge erected.

Across the bridge is the very old inn once named 'Ye Sygne of St. John Baptist Head'. The building was originally used to lodge the men working on the bridge and it was dedicated to St. John the Baptist. In 1704 the name was changed to its present, and more apt title, The Trout.

This is a pleasant place, away from the town, and it offers walks along the towpath in both directions, upstream towards Lechlade or downstream towards Buscot.

10. Buscot—lock and weir

From St. John's bridge continue along the A417 towards Faringdon for a further 1¼ miles to Buscot village. Along this route there are several signposts indicating footpaths down to the river on the left. The village was designed and laid out in 1879, the equivalent perhaps of our present day New Towns and it still has a trim, well-cared-for appearance. After turning off the main road to take the left turning through the village one can see on the right a tap in its own shelter. This source of water was provided by Squire Campbell of Buscot House. (Now the National Trust property on the right of the main road.) He installed in the Thames, after gaining Parliament's permission, a huge water wheel sixteen feet wide and twenty-five tons in weight, to pump water for his tenants, to irrigate the land and to replenish the reservoir on his estate.

On the right of the village road is a car park for visitors to the lock and weirs. Pass through the small gate and walk down the track across the field. The weir soon comes into view and a pleasant sight and sound it makes. On arrival at the lock cottage, go through the gate and follow the chain fence round the cottage. Cross the weir by bridge on to the lock island. This lock is the same age as the lock at St. John's and at five feet nine inches is one of the deepest on the river. This was the last lock on the Thames to have a full-time keeper in charge, and incidentally it was the last privately owned weir. Cross to the far bank and towpath for a mile walk downstream to Kelmscott footbridge.

11. Kelmscott footbridge, site of Anchor Inn and Kelmscott Manor

The footbridge leads on to an island on which stands a building which is now a fishing club's headquarters but was until recently a favourite 'watering' place for river users known as the Anchor Inn. Prior to this it was the weir keeper's house. Its most notorious owner 150 years ago was a Mr Hart (the area is still referred to as Hart's Weir) who decided to augment his income by smuggling. He bought kegs of spirits from bargemen and hid them on the ends of chains at the bottom of the river.

11

On the downstream end of the island on the south side below the footbridge, careful examination will reveal brickwork lining the channel, with slots to accommodate weir boards or some device to 'pound' or 'lock' the water.

12. Radcot bridges and lock

Return to the A417 and turn left towards Faringdon three miles away. In Faringdon turn left at the traffic lights on the A4095 towards Witney. Approximately 2½ miles along this road Radcot and its three bridges are negotiated. Great care is necessary here as each bridge is a potential danger spot if taken too quickly or if traffic is approaching in the opposite direction. A car park is available after crossing the first bridge, on the right in a field that is owned by the Swan Inn. The towpath runs through this field and over Cradle Footbridge and on to Radcot lock and weirs. A little further down is Old Man's Footbridge crossing the river.

The first road bridge crossed was the original bridge over the Thames navigation and was passed under by river traffic until the cut was made, under the next bridge, in 1787. The old bridge possibly dates from the reign of Henry III (1216-72) and the pedestal on the parapet probably once carried a figure of the Virgin Mary. It was also proposed at one time to build a chantry chapel on the bridge, but sufficient funds were not raised and the idea was abandoned. With modern traffic as it is it was probably a good thing, as the bridge now measures only twelve feet from side to side.

Apart from the present traffic this bridge has seen other troubled times. In 1387 the Earl of Oxford with 5,000 men were attacked by John of Gaunt's son and put to flight. The Earl escaped, it is said, by forcing his horse to leap the parapet of the bridge into the river beneath and made good his escape by swimming to the bank. The bridge was also the scene of skirmishes during the Civil War when it was held for a time for the King by forces from Faringdon.

13. New Bridge and two inns

From Radcot bridge continue north on the A4095 through Clanfield to Bampton, some four miles. In Bampton take the B4449 through Ashton for five miles until the A415 is reached. Turn right and drive towards Kingston Bagpuize for two miles to New Bridge.

This is a handsome old bridge with alcoves over the upstream buttresses, from which the Windrush can be seen flowing into the Thames from the Oxfordshire bank. Although the bridge is called New it vies with Radcot as being the oldest on the river!

It was built in 1250 and, like Radcot, was the scene of many a clash between Roundhead and Cavalier during the Civil War.

There are two inns here, one at each end of the bridge. On the Oxfordshire bank is the Rose Revived which was once an alehouse called the Chequers, then a hermitage and now an inn. Its companion on the Berkshire bank, in fact almost part of the bridge, is the Maybush, and it is beside this inn that access to the river can be gained.

14. Bablock Hythe—ferry and inn

At the Rose Revived on the A415 take the minor road behind the inn leading to Northmoor 1½ miles away, and then turn right again for Bablock Hythe.

There was a ferry here and the slipways remain on both banks. The inn beside the large parking area used to be known as the Chequers but is now more aptly, in effect rather than cause, called the Ferry. The principal reason for many of the ferries across the Thames was simply that the towpath changed banks, due to land owners' rights, and the horses had to be transported across. At Bablock Hythe, however, business developed beyond this simple function, for even in 1692 Thomas Baskervile wrote 'Bablock Hythe has a great boat to carry over carts and coaches'. Up to the mid 1960's the 'great boat' was carrying cars and passengers across until it was decided that it was unsafe and the income too small to warrant a new boat and winching gear.

The tow path follows the river upstream from the inn and it is only a walk of about two miles up to Northmoor lock and weir.

15. Eynsham—Swinford bridge and lock

From Bablock Hythe drive through West End and join the B4449 for Stanton Harcourt. Continue on this road through the village and after a drive of 3 miles Eynsham will be reached.

Eynsham is a very old village dating from 561, and in the eleventh century a Benedictine abbey was founded here, but since the Dissolution it has been lost almost without trace, though it is likely that a good number of the houses in the village are built with the stone from it.

To reach the river turn right on to the B4044 towards Oxford, a drive of about one mile. The bridge is one of only two toll bridges remaining over the Thames and it was built by the Earl of Abingdon in the late eighteenth century. The toll house is on the village side of the bridge. On this journey to the bridge two establishments have been passed, the first the Talbot, an early seventeenth century coaching inn, and the second the Swan Hotel, part of which is reputed to be the original guest house for the old abbey.

To gain access to the towpath and lock cross the bridge and park on the right. On the left between two houses and the Oxford

City Waterworks buildings is a gate and a stile. Cross the stile and follow the path to the lock. From this position an excellent view of Swinford bridge can be obtained.

16. Godstow—nunnery and lock

From Swinford Bridge drive along the B4044 towards Oxford. After 4 miles Botley will be reached where the B4044 joins the A420 to pass under the Oxford by-pass to the traffic lights. Turn left here and drive up to and round the roundabout taking the third exit. A short way along this road a minor road leaves on the left. Follow this road through Wytham and on under the by-pass to Godstow. This will easily be recognized as the nunnery comes into view on the right shortly after emerging from under the by-pass. The best parking can be found by driving over the bridges to a car park a quarter of a mile beyond the river.

Large parts of the twelfth-century nunnery walls are still standing but little effort has been made to make them look attractive and easy to view. The chapel in the south east corner is gated off.

It was at this nunnery that Rosamund was educated before King Henry II met her here on an excursion from his palace in Oxford, and fell in love with her. She left her peaceful haven by the river for him and went to Woodstock where the King could visit her often. Unfortunately Queen Eleanor discovered the alliance and the affair ended. Rosamund then returned to Godstow in penitance and died there.

Upstream from the bridge can be seen the new by-pass bridge spanning the Thames. Below the second bridge is a weir and further along is the Trout Inn. This was the guest house of Godstow nunnery. It now has an excellent car park opposite for the use of patrons. Notice also in the wall by the car park, a plaque now almost overgrown with ivy.

17. Oxford—Folly bridge and towpath

From the car park at Godstow turn away from the Thames and head for the main Woodstock to Oxford road. Passing through the city, head for the Abingdon road which crosses the Thames by means of Folly Bridge.

The bridge has an interesting history dating from the Norman period when it had eighteen arches and also a towered gatehouse on the south end. This bridge was built, over the site of a ferry, by Robert d'Oigly who also built Wallingford and Oxford castles, and it was known as Grand Pont.

Friar Roger Bacon was reputed to have used the gatehouse as a study, and it was said that if any man more learned should pass under the tower it would fall on his head. Whether or not the University authorities were worried about this is not known, but they did have the gatehouse demolished in 1779 because it was thought unsafe. This, however, occurred after Mr. Welcome had erected another storey on top of Friar Bacon's study. It was known at this time as Welcome's Folly. Nowadays Mr. Welcome has been forgotten but not his folly! The best place from which to view the bridge is down the towpath through the right hand parapet at the south end. Opposite this access point, on the other side of the bridge, is Salters' Boatyard alongside which you are almost certain to see moored at least one of their large passenger-carrying steamers. Salters have been performing a daily river service for eighty years or more and know well how to care for their passengers.

There was once a flash weir beneath the bridge and when the bridge was being rebuilt in the 1820's a shallow pound lock was constructed. This proved very inconvenient to river traffic and the gates were removed towards the end of the nineteenth century.

On the downstream side of the bridge the towpath follows the curve of the river round the regatta course, with Christchurch Meadow on the far bank. Nearly opposite Oxford University boathouse, the river Cherwell flows into the Thames.

New Bridge

15

18. Iffley—church, mill, lock and rollers

From Folly bridge drive up into Oxford and at Carfax turn right down High Street. At the roundabout, after crossing the river Cherwell, take the Henley road, the A423. After a drive of 1½ miles during which you pass the road to Donnington bridge, another access point to the river Thames, fork right for Iffley. At the T-junction turn right into the village. Continue on this road to the church masked by trees at the very end of the road. (Just before reaching the church, notice the fine old thatched school on the right.) The church is considered by many to be one of the finest examples of Norman architecture remaining. It was built in 1160 and is oblong and without aisles. Notice the magnificent zig-zag pattern and the beak heads on the west door.

The lane to the right of the church is Mill Lane which leads by a left turn down to the lock and weirs. The last dwelling on the right before the end of the lane is Grist Cottage, which is thought to be part of the old mill which was burnt down in 1908. It was a thirteenth century mill and the only visible remain we can see is the sadly neglected mill-stone placed, with a plaque, at the very bottom of the lane amongst the grass and weeds.

To the right of the stone is the path leading over the weir to the lock island. The lock was built in 1923 in what was then known as Iffley Pool. Beyond the lock is the double set of rollers, used by light craft to by-pass the lock. Over these pass two bridges to the towpath; one a rustic bridge and, at the top of the island, a fine, ornamented stone footbridge. From here it is a short and pleasant walk up to Folly bridge and Oxford.

19. Kennington and Sandford—lock, weirs and mill

From Iffley, return to the main A423 Henley/Oxford road and turn left. A short way back along here turn left again to cross Donnington Bridge over the Thames. At the traffic lights turn left and drive to the roundabout on the Oxford by-pass. Leave this roundabout by the second exit and a short distance along the by-pass turn left to join the Kennington road. In the village, on the left, will be seen the Tandem Inn, with a public car park opposite. To the right of the main building is a public footpath to the river. The path crosses the railway line by means of a very unsightly iron bridge. From here it is a very short walk to the river along any one of the many well-trodden paths across this green. Anywhere along here is a good spot for a picnic, as the railway line keeps everyone except pedestrians well away from the river. It is also a pleasant spot for walking, upstream over the Hinksey Stream or downstream to Sandford lock.

Leaving the Tandem continue on to the end of the village about a mile away and turn left at the bottom of a slope down Sandford Lane. Pass under the railway bridge and park by the river. Up to the left can be seen the lock, which is approached across a footbridge over a backwater. This is an interesting area, marred to some extent by the tall chimney of Sandford paper mill. Cross the lock and investigate the head race for the mill. This in fact was the old pound lock built by the Oxford/Burcot Commission in 1632 and was one of the earliest on the Thames. It was lengthened in 1793 and rebuilt in 1795, but this was not enough and in 1836 the present lock was built. Sometime later the mill owners purchased the old pound lock, removed the gates and fitted an extra mill-wheel in it to supply more power to the mill. The mill itself, though this is not apparent now, was built in 1294 by the Knights Templar who had a preceptory near by.

The hotel on the Oxfordshire bank is the King's Arms and it is reached by crossing the wooden bridge which was once a toll bridge.

20. Radley and Nuneham Park

Continue along the road from Kennington the 1½ miles to Radley, past Radley Large Wood and the entrance to St. Peter's College, both on the right. At the church turn left, and a little way down the village road turn left again over the railway bridge. A quarter of a mile beyond the railway the lane divides; take either route, as each returns to this point. Follow the direction of your choice until the gate leading to Radley College boathouse is encountered. Park on the verge here and walk down to the river. This is a pleasant reach with walks upstream on the towpath to Sandford lock, or downstream with Nuneham Park on the opposite bank. The latter has been the home of two great families since Roger Courtenay became the owner in 1214. In the reign of Queen Anne it was bought by the then Lord Chancellor, Simon Harcourt. It was this family who built the present house partly from stone brought here after the demolition of their previous home at Stanton Harcourt. It is of interest to note that both families have left their names in villages they once possessed; the Harcourts at Stanton Harcourt and the Courtenays at Sutton Courtenay, further downstream. The park was laid out by the renowned 'Capability' Brown.

21. Abingdon—abbey, bridge, lock and weir

Leaving the river at Radley cross back over the railway bridge and turn left for Abingdon, a journey of two miles. The town is well served with car parks, and to reach the bridge follow the Henley signs on the A415. Just before the bridge on the left is the abbey gateway leading to the abbey grounds, a recreational area and swimming pool. Immediately before crossing the bridge is, again on the left, Thames Street, at the end of which is the old mill and also what remains of the abbey buildings, which are certainly worth a visit. The abbey was founded in 675 and belonged to the Benedictine order. William the Conqueror was a guest here two years before the Domesday Book was compiled, and Henry I was educated in the abbey. In its heyday it was the second most powerful abbey in England, but like the majority of other monastic establishments, it lost almost everything at the Dissolution in Henry VIII's reign. Incidentally the abbot used to exact a toll from each river user of 100 herrings in Lent of each year!

The bridge was built in 1416 by the Guild or Fraternity of the Holy Cross to replace a ford and a ferry. There is a story about the ferry which tells of an abbot returning to the abbey in the company of monks and students. The crossing was difficult because of the flood-water coming downstream, and the ferry capsized and all were drowned. The bridge is really two bridges; from the town to the island is Abingdon bridge, and from the island to the southern bank is Burford bridge (Borough ford). The latter leads straight on to a causeway, contemporary with the bridge, which stretches for nearly a mile alongside the road to Culham. One would imagine that the drowned abbot might haunt the bridge, but this is not so. The ghost which once haunted the bridge was that of a woman. She walked the streets and the bridge, dressed in white, and during the day she was seen only as a head upon the water. She harmed no one and was only heard to say one word, 'Revenge'. The ghost was exorcised by St. John of Nepomuck, the patron saint of bridges, at the invitation of the abbot.

From the southern bank access to the towpath is available in both directions. Downstream on the opposite bank from the towpath is St. Helen's church, a famous Thames landmark, St. Helen's wharves, which once bustled with much land, river and canal traffic, the little river Ock flowing into the Thames, and round the bend beside the stone building on the river's edge, is the spot where once the Wiltshire/Berkshire Canal entered the Thames. This canal once linked with the West country by joining the Kennet and Avon Canal at Semington, and although never undertaken, it was planned to continue the canal through to Aylesbury to link with the Grand Junction, now the Grand Union Canal.

Upstream from the bridge is Abingdon lock, and beyond, by the small overflow weir, is the Swift Ditch, the story of which will be recounted later. By crossing the lock and the weir over the footbridge you will arrive at the mill stream and the abbey grounds, through which you can return to the town.

22. Culham—bridge and Swift Ditch

Crossing Abingdon bridge drive for about a mile along the A415 to Culham bridge. Immediately over the bridge turn right and park on the left hand side of the road to Culham village.

The present concrete road bridge was built in the 1930's and bears a plaque with the date. The more interesting bridge, however, is the old stone one parallel to the new and reached by the gate to the right of the village road by Toll Cottage. It was built in the fifteenth century by the same guild which built Abingdon bridge and the causeway joining the bridges. It has been patched up rather than restored on the upstream side, but it is still worthy of investigation. The best place from which to view it is across the bridge and over the stile on to the spit of land formed by deposits brought down by the river Thames. Notice the variety and shape of the arches, taking special note of the lefthand ones; these ribbed arches are probably parts of the original bridge. The centre spans were probably widened to accommodate river traffic, because although the stream which now flows under the bridge does not appear important, it is really the mainstream of the Thames.

When the monks built their abbey at Abingdon they built it over half a mile from the Thames at that time, but to power their mill, and also for the general convenience and cleanliness of the abbey, they cut a stream from the river to pass the abbey. In 1060 a navigation cut was formed beside the mill stream to serve the town of Abingdon and, as a consequence, the mainstream fell into disuse. In 1624, however, when improvements to the navigation were being made by the Oxford/Burcot Commission, it was decided to rejuvenate the Swift Ditch and make it the main stream again. A pound lock was built on this section at this time, like the one described at Sandford, and it is still in existence, though dammed at its lower end. In 1790, however, Abingdon lock was built and the navigation again resumed its 'unnatural' course by the town, leaving Swift Ditch to silt up and become overgrown.

Returning to the car the spire of St. Helen's church and the roof of County Hall in Abingdon can be seen above the trees.

23. Sutton Courtenay—lock, weirs and pools

Leaving Culham Bridge continue down the minor road to

19

Culham village past the green, with the church beyond, and up to the T-junction. Turn right to the lock on the Culham Cut which was constructed in 1809. The lock and car park are on the right. Drive from here into the village where a parking area is signposted. Walk back from the car park to the sharp right hand bend in the village. Between the end of a row of picturesque cottages and a brick wall forming a right angle at the bend in the road, is a path and footbridge over a backwater leading into the Sutton Pools area. This is a beautiful, unspoilt backwater on the Thames and contains a large area to explore. If, however, a circular walk is required, then keep to the main path across the foaming weirs and eventually on to a public footpath across a field to reach Culham Cut and a footbridge. Cross the bridge for access to the towpath and a short walk to the lock. The return journey can be taken across Sutton bridge, built in 1807 on the site of a ford. (Until 1930 a toll had to be paid here.)

Sutton Pools, once the navigation channel, powered a mill beneath which was a flash lock. This was most unusual and a constant source of complaint from bargemen having to negotiate it. The tolls for the use of it were extremely high and this was another cause for complaint. After the new cut had been completed the old mill and weirs were bought out by the Commissioners of the river for £3,000.

Sutton Courtenay village is worth investigating. It once belonged to the abbey at Abingdon as a retreat for the abbots, and later was owned by the Courtenays, (encountered earlier at Nuneham). It has a twelfth century manor house and numerous picturesque cottages and houses.

24. Clifton Hampden—lock, bridge and church

From the car park in Sutton Courtenay leave the village by the same road as you entered, across Sutton Courtenay bridge past the entrance to Culham lock, and then straight up to the main road. At the T-junction turn right past the Waggon and Horses public house and drive the 2 miles to the right turn down into Clifton Hampden village. In the village turn right to cross the fine brick built bridge. Although the bridge has a mediaeval appearance, it was built in 1864 to replace a ferry. The bed of the Thames at this point is unique in that it is solid rock— sandstone. It is this sandstone which forms a cliff on which the church is built and from which the village takes part of its name. The Hampden part of the village's name comes from the pre-Elizabethan era when the forefathers of John Hampden owned it. In fact it is said that John himself visited the village and lodged at the thatched Plough Inn on the main road.

The toll house for the bridge still stands on the far bank and beyond it is the Barley Mow Inn, an old cruck cottage at least 600 years old, where parts of *Three Men in a Boat* were written by Jerome K. Jerome.

On the left beyond the Barley Mow is a large free car park very close to the river. From here it is only a short walk back across the bridge and upstream along the towpath to Clifton lock on its cut. It took nearly thirty years to plan, purchase the land and construct this lock, because the landowner was a lunatic and the legal complications ensuing from this fact were numerous!

25. Day's lock—Sinodun hills, Dyke hills and Dorchester

At the car park at Clifton Hampden turn left along beside the Thames backwater, with a view of the lock cottage and the weir, to Long Wittenham. In this village take the left turn for Little Wittenham, just over a mile away. In Little Wittenham go left again at the T-junction. Just before the church there is a public footpath leading off to the right which is worth following. It leads through Little Wittenham Woods up to the top of Sinodun Hills. At the top is an ancient hill fort, and the view from here is worth the exertion of the climb. It gives a panoramic view of the Thames Valley all around.

From the church follow the lane to its end at a footbridge overhung with trees. This first bridge leads over a backwater to a second bridge over the weir stream, and to the lock cottage. A third bridge spans the navigation stream. The view upstream, at this point, reveals the lock and the weir, and the towpath leads down to them for a closer inspection.

From the lock, strike off in a north-easterly direction until reaching Dyke hills. These are man-made ditches and ramparts over 20 feet high in places. It is not known who built them or when, but they are certainly an interesting feature. They form a barrier between the rivers Thames and Thame to the south of Dorchester, and it may have been that the Thames water once filled the ditches to form a sort of moat. In 1870 a local farmer set idle labourers to work on levelling the ramparts, but fortunately he was soon stopped and little damage resulted. The walk can be continued into Dorchester to visit the ancient abbey, which was more fortunate than most at the time of the Dissolution. Richard Beaulieu was able to purchase it for £140, and he gave it to the parish for ever. Its history goes back to the seventh century when Cynegil, the first West Saxon king to become a Christian, was baptized here.

26. Wallingford and Crowmarsh Gifford

The road from Little Wittenham passes round the Sinodun hills and after a mile reaches a T-junction. Turn left here for Wallingford, and in half a mile the road joins the A4130 for 2½ miles into Wallingford.

This town used to be of much greater importance than may appear at the present time. The Romans, Saxons and Danes all came to Wallingford, either to sack or settle here because, as the name suggests, it was an important ford. It is an interesting fact that William the Conqueror, after the battle of Hastings, made his first crossing of the Thames here, rather than heading direct for London. It was his appointed governor of the area, Robert d'Oigly, who in 1071 had the castle built on the mound by the river (now private property). Matilda was under siege in the castle from Stephen and, in a later Civil War, Cromwell at last captured and destroyed it in July 1646. The mound and parts of the keep belonging to the castle are still to be seen from the river bank.

Wallingford's decline came about during a series of plagues in the area, and also because of the rise in importance of Abingdon. Nowadays it competes with Abingdon for popularity with the visitors to its riverside attractions and amenities. On the Crowmarsh Gifford bank it has recreational areas, swimming and paddling pools.

A bridge, so tradition says, was first thrown across the Thames here as early as A.D. 600, but there is no evidence to support this. The first known bridge was built in 1141 and, in 1809, due to extensive damage by flooding, the bridge was rebuilt and made wider. In the past it must have been a very cluttered bridge, for it is said to have supported the Mary Grace Chapel, destroyed by cannon shot from the Parliamentarians in the Civil War, a gatehouse at each end, and sluices and weirs beneath it. In 1641 Colonel Bragge removed four river arches and replaced them with a wooden drawbridge to aid the defence of the town. All have now disappeared, and we are left with a bridge forming a pleasant sweep across the river to Crowmarsh Gifford.

Crowmarsh Gifford was given to a Norman lord by the name of Gifford, who was the standard bearer to William of Normandy. Although not present himself at the battle of Hastings, two of his sons did take part. The village later became a leper colony. History has left its mark upon a door of the church in the form of two cannon ball holes made during the siege of Wallingford in the Civil War. The door formerly hung on the south side of the church, but has now been removed to form the outside door leading from the priest's sacristy.

27. Cholsey—Papist Way to ferry

Take the south road, the A329, out of Wallingford to Cholsey, a journey of less than 3 miles. At the crossroads, just past Fair Mile Hospital, turn left and drive down the lane to the river to the position where the ferry used to ply. This lane is part of the Papist Way, an ancient road which, it is thought, ran from Cholsey monastery, of which there are no visible remains, down to the Thames, across the ferry and up to Berin's Hill, three miles away on the far bank. The hill was named after St. Berin who is said to have established a cell on the top.

Cholsey monastery has an interesting story attached to it. When King Edgar died he left two sons: Edward was the elder, but Edgar had re-married and his wife, Elfthryth, thought her son, Ethelred, should be made king. He was not, so mother and son, bitterly disappointed, retired to Corfe Castle on the Isle of Purbeck. Sometime later, when Edward was out hunting alone near the castle he called there for food and shelter. Instead he received a knife in the back and he fled on his horse away from the scene of the crime, until he died from his wounds and fell from his mount. Ethelred was proclaimed king, but he never forgot the brutal murder of his step brother, and it is said he built the monastery at Cholsey as an act of repentance. The monastery had but a short existence of twenty years before, in 1006, the Danes razed it to the ground during a raid on the district.

28. Streatley and Goring

From Cholsey continue along the A329 into Streatley, and at the cross-roads turn left for the river. The towpath crosses the river at the bridge and access is available, on the Berkshire side by a path near the church, and on the Oxfordshire side at the far end of the bridge. The twin villages offer riverside walks, recreation fields and pleasure craft, as well as the magnificent view of the weirs and lock from the bridge joining the two villages.

A very enjoyable ten minute walk is to climb up the hill behind Streatley, by means of the path beside the Youth Hostel. This offers the reward of a good view of the Thames scene below and around.

The hotel in Goring called Ye Miller of Mansfield got its name, according to the legend, from the time of Henry III. The king was out hunting near Mansfield when he asked at a nearby mill for refreshment. The miller, not recognising the person as the king, and thus the only person with the right to hunt and kill deer in the forest, served venison and ale to the visitor. After the meal Henry revealed the fact that he was king to the miller, who in turn begged and pleaded for mercy. The meal must have put the king in a good humour, for he forgave the miller and offered him land in Goring for as long as he should give food and shelter to weary travellers.

While standing on the bridge watching the weirs, try and imagine the scene in 1674. There was no bridge in those times, and Goring Feast was coming to a noisy close. Sixty people clambered into the ferry boat, singing, shouting and generally making merry. They were on their way home to Streatley. The ferryman, who was probably a little drunk, ran the boat too close to the thundering weirs, the current took hold of the densely-packed boat and forced it to its doom over the weir, drowning all sixty persons on board!

29. Basildon House and Childe-Beale Wild Life Trust

Take the A329 from Streatley to Pangbourne, but after two miles on the right are the impressive lodges and gateway to the National Trust property of Basildon House, open to the public from April to the end of October. The house is built in a fine Palladian style but it has had a very chequered existence. Designed by John Carr of York and built, during the period 1776 and 1783, by Sir Francis Sykes, it suffered changes of ownership and neglect until in 1952 Lord and Lady Iliffe purchased and lovingly restored it.

From Basildon continue towards Pangbourne for half a mile and, beyond the Skew bridge, on the left stands the entrance to a drive guarded by two white stone lions.

During summer days, from Easter Sunday onwards, this drive is open to the public and winds down to the river's edge and a park area known as the Childe-Beale Wild Life Trust containing a pavilion and many statues. There are peacocks strutting about the grounds alongside other domesticated creatures such as Highland cattle, Shetland Ponies and rare British breeds of sheep.

Returning to the main road, turn left and drive the remaining two miles into Pangbourne, where, before reaching the railway bridge, by the Swan Inn car park, there is a very good view of the weirs.

30. Pangbourne and Whitchurch

In the centre of Pangbourne the main road turns sharp left. Follow this round and immediately turn left again. Just before reaching Whitchurch bridge, a toll bridge, (the charge being 4p for a car), turn right into the car park beside the boat house and

The statue of Father Thames at St John's lock, Lechlade.

Halfpenny Bridge at Lechlade was so called because of the price of the toll.

The navigational arch of Radcot Bridge.

Rushey lock is between Radcot and New Bridge.

New Bridge is actually one of the oldest on the Thames.

Swinford is one of the two remaining toll bridges over the Thames.

A backwater near Folly Bridge, Oxford.

The boat rollers and ornamental bridge at Iffley.

The tall chimney of the paper mill dominates Sandford.

Nuneham Park stands in grounds landscaped by 'Capability' Brown.

The spire of St Helen's church, Abingdon, is a famous landmark.

Sutton Pools is a beautiful, unspoilt backwater.

The Victorian brick bridge at Clifton Hampden.

Benson lock, near Wallingford.

The view from Streatley Hill looking towards Pangbourne.

A cruiser on the Thames near Pangbourne.

Sonning lock.

Temple Island at Henley is the start of the Royal Regatta course.

Hambleden Mill.

Bourne End.

Marlow.

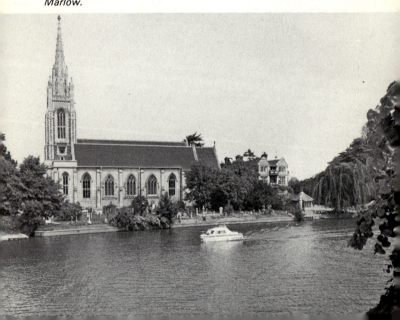

Brunel's railway bridge at Maidenhead.

Cliveden Reach where the beechwoods come down to the river's edge.

The old bridge between Windsor and Eton.

A picnic by the river at Staines.

'Swan uppers' at Cookham.

Sunbury on Thames.

recreation centre. This park gives access to the river along the towpath beside the regatta course. There is a good view upstream from the iron toll bridge.

The creator of Mr Toad, of *Wind in the Willows* fame, was closely connected with Pangbourne. Kenneth Grahame's house can be found close by the church. It is called Church Cottage, and this famous children's author died there on 5th July 1932. The tool shed belonging to the cottage was once the lock-up.

31. Mapledurham—house, village, mill and weirs

Cross Whitchurch toll bridge and continue on this road for approximately three-quarters of a mile, then take the first right (Hardwick Road) towards Goring Heath. After 1¼ miles the gates of Hardwick Hall, which Charles I was allowed to visit during his imprisonment at Caversham, will be seen ahead. Turn left and drive for over a mile until the crossroads on the B4526 is reached. Turn right here and just over 2 miles ahead lies the turning, clearly marked, down through the woods to Mapledurham. While driving down this lane it is not difficult to realise that the village at the end is going to be rather special, in that it is one of the few remaining villages almost untouched by the twentieth century.

One of the first houses, on the right, called the White House, used to be a public house called The King's Arms, and before that it was the Priest's house. A little beyond, but still on the right, is a row of almshouses dated 1613. Further down on the left is the church, built on the site of an earlier foundation. The church is unusual in that it not only houses Church of England worshippers but it also has an aisle, separated from the main church by railings, devoted to the Roman Catholic religion. This strange state of affairs came about as a result of the owners of the estate, the Blounts, being of the Catholic faith. Their home is behind the church and it can be visited between Easter and the end of September each year.

It is a fine Tudor building and its restoration is of necessity slow but, in this case, well worth while. Beside the Tudor mansion stands a smaller but much older house, now used as a tea room for visitors. Some restoration work has been done on the old corn and grist mill beyond the church by the river. This mill is the oldest still in existence on the Thames. It has been fitted with a new undershot wheel and it is open to the public to see it working. It used to have two wheels and was worked into the early years of this century. It was then adapted to pump water for the estate reservoirs and to turn a dynamo to provide the manor with electricity.

If the visitor wishes to travel to the House by river the launch *Caversham Lady* leaves Caversham Bridge on days when the House is open.

Past the mill are the weirs on the river, and across the island is Mapledurham lock.

Mapledurham House is open to the public from Easter Sunday until the end of September on Saturdays, Sundays and public holidays from 14.30 to 17.30. The watermill is open at the same times.

32. Reading

Return along the village road from Mapledurham to the B4526 and turn right. In just under a mile this road joins the B479 to Caversham. After approximately 2½ miles turn right in Caversham on to the main road crossing the bridge to Reading. There is access at this bridge to the towpath on the Berkshire side. Upstream is a pleasant open stretch of land beside the river which is ideal for walks or picnics. The towpath here follows the regatta course. Near the lock, downstream from the bridge on the Oxfordshire bank, is a pleasant area of public gardens.

Forbury Gardens, between the station and the river Kennet, is a good place to visit as it contains the remains of the Benedictine abbey, and nearby is Reading Museum which contains a collection of articles dredged up at Day's lock on the Thames further upstream.

To the north of Forbury Gardens is Reading bridge, to the right of which is Kings Mead containing the towpath and a recreation area by Caversham lock. The towpath downstream leads to the junction of the river Kennet and the Thames. There is a footbridge to carry the towpath over the Kennet.

33. Sonning—lock and bridges

Leave Reading by Caversham bridge on the A4155 to Henley.
After 2½ miles turn right on to the B478 through Sonning Eye.
Along this road, on the right, is a lane leading off between the
sand-pits on the right and the Thames on the left. This is the base
for Reading Sailing Club which uses the river and the water-filled
sand-pits. Parking is available at the end of this lane.

Further down the road in Sonning, parking is available in a
small public car park opposite the French Horn Hotel. This
cark park is beside the first of two iron bridges over the backwater and then the mill stream. A brick bridge carries the road
over the main channel, and is a narrow eighteenth century
bridge with traffic lights on it. The towpath on the village end
of the brick bridge takes the walker up to Sonning lock, many
times the winner of the Thames Conservancy Best Garden
Competition, and the weirs. Between the brick bridge and the
first iron bridge is a wooden towpath bridge across the weir-
stream and on to the towpath. This is a pleasant walk with views
of the pretty village of Sonning.

34. Lower Shiplake—lock and weirs

From the car park at Sonning return along the lane through
Sonning Eye to reach the A4155 Henley road. It is just over 2
miles to Shiplake along this road. It was in Shiplake church in
1850 that Tennyson was married. Beyond Shiplake take the first
turning on the right to Lower Shiplake. It is about half a mile
down this lane to the lock. Parking is available on the right of the
lane leading to Mill House, and nearby is the footpath giving
access to the lock and towpath. The lock is reached by means of a
footbridge over the mill stream. Downstream there is a pleasant
view towards the railway bridge, and upstream the towpath
follows the river past the head of the weirs which flow through
the backwater to Wargrave.

35. Marsh lock and bridges

From Shiplake lock return to the Henley road and turn right.
Drive for approximately 2 miles until Mill Lane is seen on the
right, just before the Henley town sign. Turn right and after
passing over the railway bridge turn immediately left into the
car park. From here it is a short walk to the river either through
the playing fields or by continuing down the lane.

A towpath walk to Henley is on the left at the river's edge.

Out over the weir stream to the lock island stretches a long wooden bridge, slightly curved. From the lock island back to the Oxfordshire bank stretches yet another, even longer curved wooden bridge. I paced the two out at 170 and 190 paces respectively. It is easy to ignore all around you while admiring the sweep of these two bridges, but while at the lock take note of the whole beautiful setting; the steep, wooded hillside on the Berkshire bank rising sharply from the river, the very attractive houses and gardens lining the banks on both sides, and the old lock cottage close by the weirs which froth and foam as the Thames water rushes over them. This perhaps forms the ideal image of the river Thames and indeed it is a very pleasant spot.

36. Henley

Return to the Henley road and turn right into Henley town. Parking places are clearly marked in the town and, as it is small, it will only be a short walk to the river. Hart Street is the main street leading from the Market Place to Henley Bridge, which is reputed to be built from stone brought here, no doubt by river, from Reading abbey. The bridge carries the sculptured heads of Isis and Thamesis above the central arch. The first bridge here was thought to have been a thirteenth century stone bridge with a chapel and an inn on it. This was followed by a wooden structure on the original stone foundations, and the present bridge was built in 1786. The Angel, between the bridge and Thames Side claims to have a stone and flint arch in the cellar which could possibly have been part of the first bridge. The Red Lion Hotel, almost opposite the Angel, was visited by Charles I in 1632 and again ten years later, and during alterations in 1889 the king's coat of arms dated 1632 was discovered over a mantelpiece.

The facilities for hiring pleasure craft at Henley are plentiful on the town side of the river, and access to the towpath can be gained from the far bank, on the left, by means of a public footpath through the Leander Club drive. This walk will take you the length of the famous Henley Regatta course, down to Temple Island, a distance of 1 mile 550 yards. One of the most exciting races this course has seen must have been during the period when the Boat Race was held here in 1843 when, because the Oxford stroke had fainted and no substitute was allowed, they had to race seven oars against the full Cambridge eight. For most of the race there was nothing between the crews, but at last Cambridge cracked, and Oxford came through to win by two lengths!

The Regatta dates from 1839 and is now a very keen international competition. In the early days, however, before the oarsmen and the crowd were so closely controlled, it must have been a chaotic affair. There would be the traditional fair with its familiar smells and sounds, the crowds surging and pushing on the bank, and the river littered with bobbing craft of all types. It is a wonder a race was ever satisfactorily completed; and to top it all the umpire was required to gallop along the river bank on horseback to keep the competing crews in view, in case his decision was required at the finish!

37. Medmenham—monument

Leave Henley on the A4155 in the direction of Marlow. Approximately 5 miles along this road will be seen, on the left, the fourteenth century inn called the Dog and Badger. Turn right and drive down Ferry Lane, parking near the river's edge.

To the left, in a private garden, is all that remains of the infamous abbey built by Italian workmen for Sir Francis Dashwood and his Monks of St. Francis. Their motto *Fay ce que voudras* indicates the activities of this fraternity not only here at Medmenham but also at the Dashwood estate at West Wycombe in Buckinghamshire. All the affairs of the club are steeped in secrecy and rumour, the truth being hard to discover, but the period after the club's foundation in 1745 is not the pleasantest period in this part of Thames history.

A footbridge across a stream to the towpath leads in a very few yards to an imposing monument. The inscription tells of the legal struggle resulting in 1899 with the courts deciding that the ferry which used to ply here should be public. Because the ferry is no longer in existence there is no means of reaching the downstream towpath, which changes sides here from the Buckinghamshire to the Berkshire side. It is possible, however, to take a walk along the upstream towpath back towards Hambleden lock.

38. Marlow and Bisham abbey

Leaving the riverside, return to the Dog and Badger on the A4155 and turn right for Marlow. The drive is little more than 3 miles and enters the town along West Street. A plaque on a house wall, up high, tells of Shelley's stay in the town in 1817. The house can be found on the left near the playing fields.

Car parking is quite well provided for in Marlow, in High Street (if you're lucky). To the left of the bridge is the parish church and it contains much of interest. A short history of the church can be purchased inside and this is worth having. Of immediate interest is the story of the piebald, or spotted, boy. This freak from the Caribbean was purchased for £2,000 and exhibited amongst the other attractions at a travelling fair, by a John Richardson of London. When the boy died early in 1813, aged four and three-quarter years, it was Richardson who had him buried in Marlow churchyard. Their combined graves can be found, much weathered, near a tree in the centre of the churchyard on the town side of the church. The stone is inscribed with a very sad poem composed by Richardson himself. In the church, just inside on the left, is a fine tablet in memory of Sir Miles Hobart, M.P. who, in a 1628 session of Parliament, locked the door of the House against the King's messenger. For this he was imprisoned in the Tower of London, and soon after his release he was killed in a coaching accident when a wheel broke as he was descending Holborn Hill. Parliament arranged the purchase and erection of the memorial in the church. Beneath the bust of the man is a picture of the accident causing his death.

In the churchyard, by the river, is a seat dedicated to the memory of a Mr. Lovell who was fond of the view at this spot. Anyone who goes there will, for certain, agree with Mr. Lovell. The view shows a full river scene from the bridge on the right, the Compleat Angler Hotel and gardens across the river, the weir waters falling away downstream, and the town of Marlow itself. The backcloth for this 'picture' is formed by the various greens of the foliage on the trees in Quarry Wood on the steep hill across the river. This wooded area is freely accessible to visitors and advantage should be taken of this opportunity to look down upon a now more mature, and certainly busier river Thames.

To reach the lock it is necessary to leave the river and the suspension bridge (which recently has been completely overhauled and restored) and to walk down Station Street turning right into Mill Lane. A footbridge leads across on to the island to the lock.

Marlow is well endowed with open spaces by the river and it is possible to walk along the towpath through Higginson Park upstream to see Bisham abbey on the far bank. This establishment was once, before Henry VIII took a hand in its affairs, a priory of Augustine canons. Later it was given to Anne of Cleves ('That great Flanders mare', as Henry VIII called her) as a gift after her divorce from the monarch. Anne gave the estate to the Hoby family and it was during their ownership of the estate that the ghost first made itself known. A Lady Hoby is said to have scolded her son and locked him away in an airless room, because he had literally blotted his copybook. When she returned later he was dead. Her ghost is said to be seen still wandering the corridors wailing and washing her hands in a bowl which has nothing supporting it! Some confirmation of this sad episode occurred much later when the blotted copybooks of a child were discovered under the floorboards in a small room.

The abbey is now used by the Central Council for Physical Recreation.

39. Hurley—inn, church, monastery buildings

Cross the suspension bridge at Marlow and continue along the main road to the roundabout. Taking the third exit, head towards Reading, but only as far as the next roundabout where the road, the A423, to Henley leaves on the right.

One mile along this road you come to a turning on the right to Hurley. On the right along this short drive to the river is Ye Olde Bell which claims to be one of the oldest inns in the country and dates back to 1135 when it was the guest house for the monastery. Parking is available to the west of the church at the end of the lane on a grassy stretch. Before seeking the river look round at the wonderful old buildings surrounding the car park. Most of them at one time were connected with the monastery. The church of St. Mary, although much restored, was built in 1086, and to the north of this is the cloister court of the monastery. Opposite these is the refectory, and to the west two barns and a dovecote. The dovecote is scheduled as an ancient monument. In a crypt, in this area, covered by an inscribed flagstone, were found three bodies dressed in Benedictine habits.

Leading from the car park are paths to the riverside; the one close to the church leads by means of a steep footbridge to the lock. The backwaters are quiet and beautiful here and it is a pleasant walk along the island, past the bathing place, to the downstream footbridge. Return towards Marlow on the A404 and at the first roundabout take the second exit to by-pass the town.

MARLOW TO WINDSOR

40. Boulter's lock and gardens

The exit from the Marlow by-pass is on the left, signposted Marlow and Bourne End, shortly after crossing the new bridge over the Thames. Having left the by-pass, at the head of the slip road turn right for Bourne End.

After driving 3 miles through Bourne End, where there is a popular sailing reach on the Thames, the river is crossed at Cookham. At Cookham, a pretty village, is a lock and weir with bathing and paddling facilities nearby. Across the Victorian iron bridge, which until recently was a privately owned toll bridge, the road continues for a further 2 miles to Boulter's Lock. The lock cannot be missed as the road runs beside the river for some distance along this reach and, as it is a popular spot for the people of Maidenhead, in fine weather the crowd will usually mark the site of the lock! A bridge over the navigation leads to an island laid out with gardens and to the weir on the right at the head of the island.

Continue into Maidenhead on the A4 towards Slough and cross the river, but immediately turn right parallel to the river. Ahead is Brunel's famous railway bridge. It is built of brick and can still claim to have the longest unsupported span, for this type of bridge, in the world. It is 128 feet in length.

41. Bray lock and weirs

From here return to the A4 towards Slough, but half a mile after passing under the railway bridge turn right, at the signpost for Dorney Reach. Along this road take the right turn down Old Marsh Lane and, just before the M4 is reached, drive down the dirt track leading off on the right. This is not a very long lane and leads directly on to the towpath where, to the right, a small field has been set aside as a car park. From this point the downstream view displays the M4 bridge over the Thames, and upstream lies Bray Lock and weirs. By walking across the lock, the island and the lock cottage can be reached, but it is not possible to walk from the far side of the island across the weirs to the millstream. Beyond the millstream lies the village of Bray well known for its unsettled vicar, Simon Alleyn. There are rewarding walks along the towpath from the lock.

42. Boveney—lock, rollers and church

Return along Old Marsh Lane to Dorney Reach road and turn right. The road crosses over the motorway, M4, and into Dorney, a distance of about a mile. In the village turn right at the T-junction and on the Common fork right and drive to the gates of 'The Old Place'. There is a small parking area to the right, and from this position the Round Tower of Windsor Castle can be seen above the trees to the south east. There are two public footpaths directing the visitor to the river and lock, the one by The Old Place being short and rather uninteresting. The other path, however, leads from the right hand corner of the parking area beside the hedge, and after a few yards it is surprising to find that just off the path to the left is a chapel. This should be investigated, and if it is locked the key may be obtained from The Old Place. The chapel is dedicated to St. Mary Magdalene, and it stands on a site which has been used as a place of worship since before the Norman Conquest. The present building is thirteenth century and was probably used by bargees when there were busy wharves nearby. The chapel is lit only by candlelight and heat is supplied by portable oil heaters: a delightful chapel on a tree-shrouded site. Continue the walk through the spinney

to the river and turn left along the towpath to the lock. On the far side of the lock is a single set of rollers for use by light craft wishing to avoid the lock. The return journey to the car is accomplished along a gravel lane leading from the lock to The Old Place.

43. Windsor

Drive back along the B3026 to Eton and across the river to Windsor, a journey of 3 miles. It is an interesting drive as glimpses of Windsor Castle are frequently caught across the river and through the trees. In Eton the road passes close by the famous College buildings dating from as early as 1441.

The bridge over the river Thames at Windsor was built in 182 and has cast-iron arches on granite piers. The earliest bridge here must have been in the thirteenth century as a grant of oak trees from Windsor Forest was recorded for its repair in 1242. Over the bridge and commanding the river rises the most majestic of all the royal palaces. Begun by William, Duke of Normandy, it has been restored, rebuilt and added to throughout the centuries, and yet it looks a complete, finished article not at all the piecemeal group of buildings it might have been.

Windsor, in common with all the other larger towns on the banks of the Thames, serves the visitor to the town and the river well. There are ample car parks, all signposted, and the riverside is easily accessible. Once at the riverside the availability of walks or the hire of pleasure craft is plentiful. Perhaps Windsor is too successful, or perhaps too famous—it certainly gets far too crowded for the real enjoyment of the Thames, especially at weekends and holiday times.

WINDSOR TO TEDDINGTON

44. Old Windsor lock
From Windsor bridge turn left on to the A328 which, if not the shortest route, is a pleasant drive through Home Park, across the river and then following the river round and crossing it again at the ornamental stone bridge, Albert Bridge. From this point and to the outskirts of Old Windsor, the road leaves the river, so turn left approximately 2 miles from the bridge down Church Road. Parking is available in the lane by the church, and from here continue on foot past the church and house under over-hanging hedges to the river. (This path can be muddy during wet weather.) At the river there are two alternatives, to continue straight on down the towpath, or to turn left upstream to Old Windsor lock, where access is permitted to the island and the backwater beyond. This lock was the first to be renovated after the war and it lacks the beauty of most of the others, there being an absence of grass and a surfeit of concrete. Downstream from the lock is the small island called Friday Island.

45. Old Windsor—Bells of Ouzeley and ferry
From the top of Church Road turn left on to the A308 into Old Windsor. The main road approaches steadily closer and closer to the river here, until just before reaching the Bells of Ouzeley, an hotel, it is between the river and the houses. The hotel therefore will be seen on the right. In front of the hotel is the ferry to carry passengers across to Wraysbury on the far bank.

The original inn on this site was built in 1150, but the present building dates only from 1936. In by-gone times it was a haunt for highwaymen taking time off from their profession in Windsor Forest. It took its present name after the time of the Dissolution when, it is said, bells from an abbey at Ouzeley were brought down the river to this point on a raft. They were then buried somewhere around this locality, but why or where is not known!

46. Runnymede and Magna Carta Island

Continuing along the A308 for a further half mile or so brings you to a car park serving the area on the Surrey bank known as Runnymede, and almost opposite the end of the car park, near the far bank is Magna Carta Island. Which of the two places was the scene of the great meeting which resulted in King John signing the Magna Carta is not known, but there is a cottage on the island containing a large flat stone reputed to be the one on which King John rested the Charter whilst signing and setting his seal on it.

Runnymede is still a good place for walking and viewing the places of interest. There is the John Kennedy Memorial and further away from the river, on the top of Cooper's Hill is the R.A.F. memorial. Incidentally, turn and admire the river view from this hill.

47. Bell Weir lock and the London Stone

Continue along the A308 to the roundabout at the far end of Runnymede, and take the first exit on the left to pass over the bridge towards Hythe End.

The towpath is accessible on both sides of the bridge on the Surrey side. A walk upstream will lead you to Bell Weir lock and rollers, passing the Angler's Hotel on the way. The lock takes its name from Charles Bell who was the first lock-keeper here in 1817, the date the lock was first built. Further along the towpath is the Egham Urban District Council bathing place, situated in a large bend in the Thames.

Downstream from the bridge brings you to a place opposite the London Stone, situated on the far bank in Ashby Recreation ground, between the two large islands. This stone was erected in 1285 and marked the former limit of control of the City of London, and from this point upstream the Thames Conservators were responsible for the river. It is thought that the stone gave the town of Staines its name.

48. Penton Hook—lock, weirs and islands

In Hythe End at the roundabout take the exit marked B376 to Laleham. One mile along this road it crosses the A30, but remain on the B376 until the turning marked Wheatsheaf Lane is observed on the right. The first turning off Wheatsheaf Lane, on the left, is Penton Hook Road. Drive to the end of this short road and park at the kerbside. (The road terminates at the towpath.) To the right the towpath leads back towards Staines and to the left is Penton Hook. The original course of the river Thames here is more than hook shaped; it is rather like a horseshoe with an extraordinary narrow opening. What the river could not do man has achieved, and the river, by means of a short cut, now flows straight across the gap in the 'horseshoe'. Fortunately, however, the water still flows round the Hook and a very popular and picturesque place it is for walks and picnics. Access to what is now an island is gained by walking across the lock gates. Beyond lie a series of weirs, each with a bridge to cross. During the Great Plague this area of land was used as a burial ground, but this fact does not seem to dissuade many people from enjoying the area.

49. Laleham House grounds and Walton Bridge

From Wheatsheaf Road turn right on to the B376 and drive into Laleham. Just past the church, which is on the left, look out for a turning to the right, opposite the Three Horseshoes, called Ferry Lane. At the fork bear right for the river and Chertsey. This road runs alongside the river Thames for over $1\frac{1}{2}$ miles with just a grass strip between them. On the left of the road are Laleham House grounds. These are now open to the public, and they form a wide tree-covered area of land with direct access across the road to the river. This is a very popular spot, and understandably so. Towards Chertsey is the lock, again by the road, with the weir beyond. Just past the lock, at the T-junction, turn left on to the B375 towards Walton. After a distance of 3 miles the A244 is reached. Turn right and within half a mile there is Walton bridge which was built in 1863, the centre arch of the previous brick bridge having collapsed in 1859. Close by the bridge at Cowey Stakes a ford existed, and as early as the eighth century its curved path across the river was marked out by stakes. The last of these were removed at the beginning of the last century as they formed a hazard to navigation. Legend has it that Caesar and his Roman legions forded the river here after a battle with Cassivillanus and his warriors. During an archaeological dig here in 1879 many British weapons were uncovered which may help to prove that the legend is true.

50. Hampton Court and bridge

On the Surrey side of Walton Bridge take the main road to the left, and in half a mile turn left on to the B370. This leads into

Hurst Road and it passes between grassy banks hiding some of the many reservoirs in this area of London. Greater London is supplied with two thirds of its water from the river Thames. Beyond the reservoirs is West Molesey and further along, until quite recently, were the grandstands of Hurst Park racecourse, now a housing estate. The T-junction ahead is the A309, crossing Hampton Court bridge. To the left on this Surrey side is the towpath up to Molesey lock and weirs. Across the bridge on the right is Hampton Court Palace, a great attraction to visitors to the metropolis. The palace park is bounded by a great curve in the Thames from Hampton Court bridge, a handsome brick and stone structure, round to Kingston bridge. The palace was built by Cardinal Wolsey for himself and his family. Henry VIII, however, took an immediate liking to the place and consequently he was soon accepting it as a gift from the Cardinal! The sovereigns of England used the palace until George III's time, and the royal apartments and the gardens are now open to the public.

51. Bushey Park and Teddington Locks

From Hampton Court drive along the A308 to the entrance to Bushey Park. This is a Royal Park and the gates are closed to the public at certain times. It is a peaceful drive through the Park after the bustle of London's more major roads. A little way into the Park is the Diana Fountain, making a very pleasing round-about in the road. Watch out also for the herd of tame deer which roams at will.

On leaving the Park turn left and almost immediately right for Teddington. At the major cross-roads in Teddington cross straight over to the minor road and park at the kerbside. Ahead and slightly to the right is the footbridge over to the islands and Teddington locks. These locks form the largest locking system on the river. There are three; the barge lock which is 650 feet long, the launch lock, (the original one was built of timber in 1811) and the skiff lock, built in 1858. The last one is sometimes known as the 'coffin' due to its shape and size. The footbridge gives access to the towpath on the far bank and along this in a down-stream direction, about a furlong from the locks, will be found a boundary stone, marking the termination of the Thames Conservancy's authority and the beginning of the section of the Thames under the jurisdiction of the Port of London Authority.

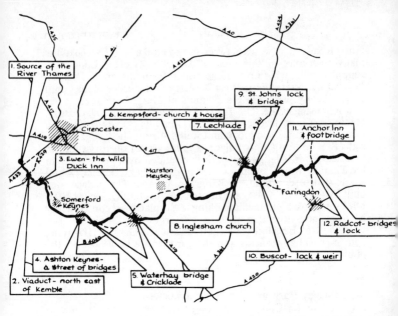

1. Source of the River Thames
2. Viaduct - north east of Kemble
3. Ewen - the Wild Duck Inn
4. Ashton Keynes - a Street of bridges
5. Waterhay bridge & Cricklade
6. Kempsford - church & house
7. Lechlade
8. Inglesham church
9. St John's lock & bridge
10. Buscot - lock & weir
11. Anchor Inn & foot bridge
12. Radcot - bridges & lock

These maps show the locations of the fifty places mentioned

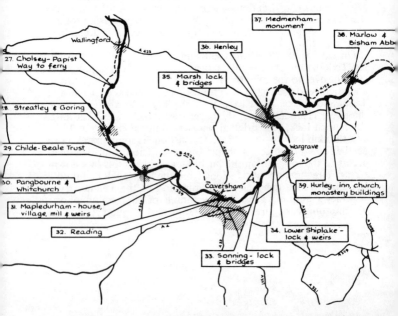

27. Cholsey - Papist Way to ferry
28. Streatley & Goring
29. Childe - Beale Trust
30. Pangbourne & Whitchurch
31. Mapledurham - house, village, mill & weirs
32. Reading
33. Sonning - lock & bridges
34. Lower Shiplake - lock & weirs
35. Marsh lock & bridges
36. Henley
37. Medmenham - monument
38. Marlow & Bisham Abbey
39. Hurley - inn, church, monastery buildings

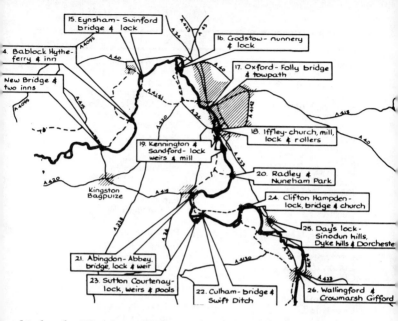

15. Eynsham – Swinford bridge & lock

4. Bablock Hythe – ferry & inn

New Bridge & two inns

16. Godstow – nunnery & lock

17. Oxford – Folly bridge & towpath

19. Kennington & Sandford – lock weirs & mill

18. Iffley – church, mill, lock & rollers

20. Radley & Nuneham Park

Kingston Bagpuize

24. Clifton Hampden – lock, bridge & church

25. Day's lock – Sinodun hills, Dyke hills & Dorchester

21. Abingdon – Abbey, bridge, lock & weir

23. Sutton Courtenay – lock, weirs & pools

22. Culham – bridge & Swift Ditch

26. Wallingford & Crowmarsh Gifford

n this book. The dotted line shows the route followed.

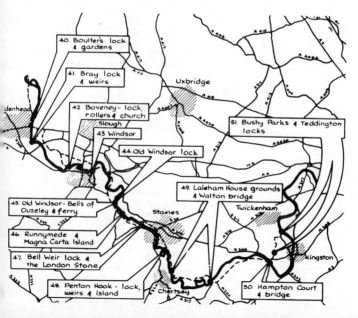

40. Boulter's lock & gardens

41. Bray lock & weirs

Uxbridge

42. Boveney – lock, rollers & church

Slough

43. Windsor

51. Bushy Parks & Teddington locks

44. Old Windsor lock

denhead

49. Laleham House grounds & Walton bridge

Twickenham

45. Old Windsor – Bells of Ouzeley & ferry

Staines

46. Runnymede & Magna Carta Island

47. Bell Weir lock & the London Stone

Kingston

48. Penton Hook – lock, weirs & island

Chertsey

50. Hampton Court & bridge

INDEX

Books by Lavinia Lewis

Shifters' Haven

Luke's Surprise
Cody's Revelation
Kelan's Pursuit
Aaron's Awakening
Nate's Deputy
Gregory's Rebellion
Pete's Persuasion
Tristan's Despair

Desert Sanctuary

An Improbable Wolf
An Indoctrinated Man

The Vanderguard Vampires

Blood Ties

Single Titles

Bollywood Desires
Too Many Chances

Too Many Chances

ISBN # 978-1-78651-931-3

©Copyright Lavinia Lewis 2016

Cover Art by Posh Gosh ©Copyright 2016

Interior text design by Claire Siemaszkiewicz

Pride Publishing

Published in 2016 by Pride Publishing, Newland House, The Point, Weaver Road, Lincoln, LN6 3QN, United Kingdom.

Printed in Great Britain by Clays Ltd, St Ives plc
1

TOO MANY
CHANCES

LAVINIA LEWIS

Dedication

Huge thanks go to Adriana for all your helpful comments, and to the readers that continue to support me. I truly appreciate you all.

Chapter One

Matt Jacobs was not having a good day.

Normally, he would say he was having a bad day — a *very* bad day — but the new positive thinking course he'd just paid three hundred bucks for forbade the use of the word bad. What would his mentor say if he used the word shitty instead? That had to be allowed, right? He was having a shitty day. *Shitty…* He turned the word over a few times in his mind. Yeah, that might work.

It wasn't like Matt had a sixth sense about these things, but from the moment he'd woken up, he'd had a feeling the day was going to suck. It had turned out to be far worse than he could have imagined.

He would have been okay about the boiler finally giving up the ghost if it hadn't happened in the middle of his shower when he was covered in soap. He *might* have been okay about the kettle blowing, but with having no coffee in his system when his crotchety old neighbour Mr Phelps cornered him on the way to his car and informed him that he was taking ownership of Snowy, Matt finally blew his top.

"The hell you are!" he fumed, glaring at Mr Phelps' snooty-assed face. "You can't just *take* my cat!"

Mr Phelps cocked an eyebrow. "Look, let's be honest here. We both know Snowy likes me better than you."

"You bought him with treats and catnip!"

Mr Phelps sniffed. "I resent that accusation."

"I don't give a rat's ass what you resent. You can't have him — he's mine."

"When was the last time he spent the night at your house?"

Matt pursed his lips and cocked his head to the side while he tried to think about the answer. It had been a while. "He goes out at night," he said at last.

"No," his neighbour corrected. "He sleeps with me."

Matt gasped. "You… You catnapper!"

Mr Phelps ignored the comment and looked over Matt's shoulder. "Ah, here he is now. Why don't we ask him?"

Matt had already agreed before he realised what a really fucking stupid idea that was. But as Snowy strolled in their direction, Matt felt the insane desire to get one up on the insufferable old coot who was looking at his cat with a deep sense of satisfaction.

"Snowy!" Matt called. "Come here, boy!"

The white tom padded up the sidewalk and into Mr Phelps' garden without so much as a sideways glance in Matt's direction. His jaw hit the ground.

"I think that settles it, don't you?" Mr Phelps said, turning on his heel and following Snowy into his house, signalling the end of their conversation.

Matt stared after them open-mouthed. He'd be pissed as all hell if he weren't so upset. He loved that damn cat.

Traitor.

The day went from bad to worse when Matt arrived at work. He was just about to get up from his desk and finally make his first cup of coffee of the morning when he heard the dreaded words.

"Matt! Get your ass in here and help me clear up this goddamn mess!"

He massaged his temples with his thumb and forefinger, trying to alleviate some of the pressure that had been building all morning. He was going to get a migraine, he just knew it. *No. Positive, Matt. Positive.*

"Matt!"

"I'm coming, sir!"

With a weary sigh, Matt got up from his desk and took the four steps needed to walk the length of his office. He crossed the small hallway and knocked on his boss' open door, hovering for a few seconds before entering. Jerry tore his gaze from the papers on his desk and glared at Matt.

"Well? What the hell you waiting for? Get your ass in here."

Jerry Gardner was a squat man in his mid-fifties with a combover and bad breath. He wore brown polyester suits that were a size too small and he was always sweating. It could be five below and Jerry would still be wiping his forehead with the same yellowing handkerchief and complaining it was a hot one. *You need this job, you need this job*, Matt repeated over and over like a mantra as he took a seat in the folding lawn chair opposite the hobbit.

Jerry popped an antacid pill then leant back in his chair, lips pursed.

"We're fucked," he said succinctly.

Matt didn't reply. He'd learnt the hard way not to interrupt his boss before he'd said what he had to say.

When the phone on Jerry's desk starting ringing he reached for it with his chubby, overly hairy fingers and barked into the receiver, "Hello!"

Matt's shoulders slouched and he leant back in his chair — not too far back because he'd learnt the hard way about doing that, too. Twice the chair had folded and he'd landed flat on his ass. It wouldn't happen a third time.

"What the fuck? Marge, I'm at *work*! I don't give a goddamn what you make for dinner, got it?"

Jerry hung up then turned his cold, beady gaze on Matt. "Where were we?"

"Uh, fucked?" Matt offered.

"Right. And do you know *why* we're fucked?"

Matt was fairly certain the question had been rhetorical but he answered it anyway. "Would it have anything to do with the Hugo-Martinez account, sir?"

"You bet your ass it would. When those fuckers backed out on the contract it left us bent over backwards and screwed up the Jacksie. You have any idea what we can do about it?"

"Sue?"

Jerry's face turned puce. "No, we can't fucking sue—and why not? Because the fuckers didn't sign anything! Don't you know a verbal agreement is not worth the paper it's written on?"

Matt was tempted to point out the inaccuracy in that statement but he valued his life too much. "So what *can* we do, sir?"

Jerry grinned. The action exposed uneven, yellowing teeth and somehow served to make him look even more unfriendly. "We grab 'em by the gonads and squeeze, that's what we do. Get 'em where it hurts, you got that?"

"Sure, sir—grab 'em and squeeze. Got it."

"Good, now get to work."

"Sir?"

Jerry looked up from his desk and scowled. "You still here?"

"Uh, just what do you want me to squeeze?"

"Are you mentally retarded?" Jerry asked.

Matt was sure he saw a blood vessel in Jerry's head pop. *Just hold it together, Matt. Don't rise to it.*

"I just told you what to do! You have to get 'em where it hurts. You telling me you don't know what would hurt Hugo and Martinez?"

Matt didn't like the sound of that one little bit. "The Hillside account, sir?"

"You're damn straight." There was another inaccuracy that Matt had no intention of correcting. He didn't want to be the cause of Jerry's sudden heart failure. He needed his job to cover his mortgage until he could find something with better pay and prospects, but the search was proving more difficult than he'd anticipated. The job was always supposed to have been temporary, a stopgap. It was meant to have been somewhere he could learn all he could about the investment business then move on. Two years later he was still putting up with Jerry's shit. He didn't know how much more he could take.

Not much.

Matt nodded and went back to his office. Jerry had been trying to procure the Hillside account for three months, but their negotiations had turned stale. The simple fact was that Jerry wasn't offering enough money to purchase the account and, short of performing a miracle, there wasn't a lot Matt could do. He'd tried on several occasions to talk his boss into raising his offer, but Jerry had shot him down every time. Jerry was too stingy for his own damn good. Matt was sure they'd get news any day informing them that Hugo and Martinez had bought the Hillside account, and that day couldn't come quick enough for him. Sure, he'd be losing out on a large commission, but he'd gone past caring. His heart wasn't in the job anymore, not that it ever really had been.

About two hours later, Matt was knee-deep in manila folders and no closer to finding a solution when his cell phone rang. He glared at the offending object, debating whether or not to answer, when Jerry's fat face appeared at his door.

"You gonna get that or do you plan on staring at it all day?"

"Of course, sir," Matt ground out. *Breathe.*

"I hope it's not a personal call. You know how I feel about personal calls at work."

"I do, sir." Matt reached across the desk and picked up his cell. There was no number on the small screen. He waited a beat, but when Jerry didn't move from the door he answered the call. "Hello?"

"Can I speak to a Mr Matt Jacobs, please?"

"Speaking. May I ask who's calling?"

"Of course, my name is Dr Mandy Coulter. I'm sorry to trouble you if you're at work, Mr Jacobs, but I'm calling from the hospital. Your father was brought in this afternoon and he had you listed as next of kin."

Matt sucked in a sharp breath. He hadn't spoken to his father in two years, but the news still made his stomach lurch and his hands break out into a sweat. "What happened to him?"

"He had a cardiac arrest."

Matt's heart started beating so damn fast he thought it was going to burst right out of his chest. *A heart attack?* "Is he going to be okay?"

The line was quiet for a moment and then the doctor spoke. "I'm afraid not, sir. I'm sorry to tell you that your father passed away about an hour ago."

Matt swallowed down the lump in his throat and managed to choke out a reply. "I see. Thank you for letting me know."

"Would it be possible for you to come to the hospital to collect your father's personal effects?"

Matt nodded then realised the doctor was still waiting for a reply. "Of course. It's a few hours' drive, but I can be there by late afternoon or early evening if that's okay." It was actually over a five-hour drive, but if he left straight away he'd be there long before nightfall.

"That would be fine, sir, thank you."

"Can I see him?" As soon as he had asked the question, Matt had second thoughts. Did he really want to see his father like that? But it was too late—the words were already out of his mouth, and like it or not, he knew it was something he had to do. He needed to see the old man with his own eyes, and he needed to say goodbye.

"Of course, and you have my sincerest apologies."

"Thank you."

It was only after he had hung up that Matt realised Jerry was still hovering inside the door. He'd completely forgotten his boss had been standing there. He ignored him while he grabbed his wallet from the drawer in his desk and his jacket from the back of his chair, mindlessly slipping his arms into it.

"I have to go home," he said at last, meeting his boss's inquisitive gaze. "My father has passed away."

"Uh, sorry about that," Jerry said, shifting awkwardly

from foot to foot. He rubbed the back of his neck then seemed to make up his mind about something. "Will you be back in the morning? We've got to get things moving on the Hillside account. We've been dragging our heels on this deal for too long."

That was about all Matt could take. He glared at his boss, his anger quickly rising to the surface. "We?" he said indignantly. There was only one person in the room who had been dragging his heels and it wasn't Matt. "There is no *we*. We haven't procured the Hillside account because *you* are too goddamn tight to pay them what they want. It's a fair price they're asking. And you know what? Fuck the Hillside account! I don't give a shit about it anymore. I just told you I lost my father. Where the hell is your compassion?"

Jerry's mouth fell open, making him look more like a guppy than he usually did. He fished the dirty handkerchief out of his pocket and swiped it across his sweaty brow. Matt regretted his outburst at first, but when Jerry next met his gaze with something bordering on hatred in his eyes, he didn't regret a damn thing.

"How dare you speak to me like that?" Jerry shrieked. "You'd better mind your mouth if you want to keep your job, boy!"

Matt had a blinding moment of clarity when he looked at his boss and knew exactly what he had to do. Calmly, he slipped his cell phone into his beat-up old briefcase and clicked it shut before striding out of the office. The pungent smell of sweat reached his nostrils as he brushed past his soon-to-be-ex boss.

"Actually, I don't want to keep it," Matt said, feeling braver with each passing second. "You can stick your shitty job where the sun doesn't shine. I quit."

Matt pulled his shoulders back, held his head high and kept on walking until he was out the door. Quitting his job was something he should have done a long time ago. He felt a stabbing pang of guilt that it had taken something as devastating as the news of his father dying to open his eyes to his situation and the choices he had made in life. He'd been a coward. He didn't know what the future held, but as he marched out to the parking lot to retrieve his car, he was sure he'd made the right decision, even if he had made it too late.

* * * *

Matt thought about his father as the familiar neighbourhoods flitted past the window during his drive home. Hank had been a stubborn man. He and Matt hadn't spoken since Matt had finally plucked up the courage to tell him he was gay and Hank had ordered him out of the house. That had been two years ago. The saddest part was that Matt knew his father would have come around, given time. He usually did when he got a bee in his bonnet about something. Matt being gay might have been a big issue to Hank, but it hadn't been so big that his father would never have got over it. At least Matt didn't think so. Hank hadn't been a prejudiced man, not really. Matt suspected that what had rankled was Hank feeling as though he had been the last person to find out.

Matt parked the car outside his house and killed the engine. He sat there for a moment and made himself take a succession of deep breaths to calm his nerves before he went inside to pack a bag. He had argued with his father countless times in the past. Their personalities were similar and they had often come to blows. But this time Matt hadn't contacted his father to find out if he had calmed down and was ready to talk to him. Matt had inherited his father's stubborn streak and it seemed neither he nor his father had been prepared to make the first move. Now Matt would never get the chance to make things up with the old man, and the harshness of that fact made his chest feel tighter and tighter until he had to close his eyes as though he could hide from the pain of it.

When he got inside, he grabbed his old suitcase out of the closet and filled it mindlessly, not even remotely aware of what he was packing. Ten minutes later he looked down, surprised to see that the case was full. Now that the adrenaline had worn off, Matt felt exhausted and he wanted nothing more than a drink or two to take the edge off the pain in his chest that wouldn't abate. He wanted to get blind, filthy drunk to be exact. He wanted to forget, to numb his feelings or to make it so that he didn't feel anything at all. He seriously considered the idea and might have given in to the temptation if he hadn't promised the doctor he'd go to the hospital later that afternoon. The long drive ahead of him meant he couldn't take the risk of having even one drink to calm him. But there would be nothing to stop him after he'd been to the hospital. As soon as the thought occurred, he ran downstairs to grab a bottle of whisky he'd had sitting around since last Christmas and stuffed it into his case between a multitude of shirts and too many socks.

Finally Matt zipped up the case, set it down in the middle of the bedroom floor and stared at it. He'd never felt so lost or so completely out of his element before. Hank had been Matt's last living relative and the bleak veracity of being all alone in the world threatened to overwhelm him. He just wished he knew why this had happened. Why now? Why at all? Matt had argued many times with his father over the years, and Hank had always had to have the last damn word. Well, he'd got it this time, hadn't he? Matt checked his watch and realised nearly two hours had passed since he'd left work. Where the hell had the time gone? He needed to get on the road if he wanted to make it to Missouri before dark.

The cell phone buzzing in his pocket snapped Matt back to reality. He fished it out and stared at the number. Tom. How could he have forgotten to call Tom? Matt thought his boyfriend should have been the first thing on his mind when he'd got the news about his father, but he was just about to drive out of state and he hadn't even paid him a second thought. He had to wonder what that said about the nature of their relationship.

Okay, so Matt couldn't really call Tom his boyfriend. They were fucking. Had been for the past five months. Matt had hoped it would lead to something more, that the more time they spent together, the more Tom would come around to the idea of them becoming a permanent couple. Tom was the closest Matt had *ever* come to having a real boyfriend, so he used the term whenever he could. Even if he couldn't say it in public because Tom wasn't out yet, he could say it in his own damn home when there was no one around to hear him. He picked up the call.

"Tom?"

"I'm really sorry, Matt," Tom began. Matt scrunched his eyebrows together and stared at his cell in confusion. How the hell had Tom found out what had happened?

"Huh?"

"I know I was supposed to be there an hour ago, but I got held up."

"Oh." It took Matt a moment before he remembered their plans for dinner. Well, the plan had been for him to cook dinner. They never went out to eat because Tom didn't like them to be seen in public together. "That's okay. Look, I've—"

"Actually that's a lie," Tom interrupted. "I didn't get held up... I mean, I did, but to tell you the truth, I wasn't planning on coming to dinner tonight."

"You weren't?"

"No." Matt heard the sharp intake of breath and waited for the rest of the words. "I had to meet with my fiancée's parents."

"Oh, that's nice," Matt replied, scrubbing a hand over his tired eyes. Then Tom's words sank in, *really* sank in. "Wait a minute, what did you just say?"

Tom let out a long sigh. "I said I had to meet with my fiancée's parents."

Matt shook his head to clear it. "But, what does that mean? I... I don't understand."

"I'm engaged, Matt."

"Yeah, I got that part. To whom and how?"

"Her name is Lindsay Rose. Our parents play golf together."

"Golf," Matt repeated dumbly. Even as he let Tom's words permeate, Matt still couldn't allow himself to believe them.

"I realise it might seem kind of sudden, but we have been seeing each other a couple of months."

Matt's stomach lurched at the admission. "Oh."

"Well, yeah, I mean... You didn't think we were exclusive or anything, did you?"

"No," Matt whispered. "Of course I didn't."

"Oh, well, that's good. I think we'll be a good match. Her father is head of the Smithsdale Corporation."

Now it all made sense. Tom worked for the Smithsdale Corporation as a junior analyst. He'd been trying to get ahead in the company for some years. Marrying the boss's daughter was bound to enhance his chances. That might be cynical, but Matt felt entitled. "That's great," he deadpanned.

"Matt? You are okay with this, aren't you?"

Matt had the insane urge to laugh, even though nothing about the situation was funny. *Was* he okay with this? Did he have any fucking choice? "Yeah, Tom, I'm just great," he managed to reply. "I've gotta go. See you around or...not."

Matt hung up and tossed the phone on the bed. It was too much. It was all too much. His pop, Tom, his damn cat. How much more could one person be expected to take in one day? Matt walked calmly into his bathroom, closed the door then threw up in the toilet. While he sat on the floor, hugging the porcelain, he wondered what his positive thinking mentor would say about his 'not good' day now.

* * * *

James looked at the picture on the menu with raised eyebrows. "You want the triple chocolate fudge sundae with marshmallows and chocolate sprinkles? That's a whole lot of chocolate for such a small girl. You sure you can fit it all in?"

Hope nodded enthusiastically, but it was the nod of approval from her mother that James made sure to get before taking the order for the calorie-laden treat. His sister would give him holy hell if he got Hope something like that without clearing it with her first.

"Two spoons, please," Maria said, much to her daughter's obvious chagrin.

James chuckled. "Yes, ma'am. Coming right up."

He went back behind the counter, gave the order to his chef Anthony and made the drinks while he waited. It had been a long, busy day. James felt like he'd worked all week and it was only Monday—not even four o'clock. He had a feeling it was going to be one of those weeks. The mall across the street opened late on Mondays and people always piled in afterwards for coffee and soda while they rested their shopped-out feet. Angela, James' assistant manager, would be arriving later to help out, but until then he was on his own out front. Not that he minded working alone, especially when it was quiet. The quiet periods gave him time to think. He often whiled away the hours on his quiet days in a seat near the window, watching the world go by. It made him happy to people-watch... Well, as happy as he could be in a town where he could never truly be himself. But those small moments of happiness were all anyone got, weren't they? No one James knew was happy all the time. He pushed the thought out of his mind and concentrated on the drinks.

He had no reason to be ungrateful for his lot. James had a good life in Providence. It might not be the life he'd always thought would be his, but it was a good life just the same. The diner had gone from strength to strength since he'd bought it five years ago and he was happy working there.

His family had believed him crazy to buy a building that needed so much work, but James had seen the potential and he hadn't been wrong. He'd used all the inheritance money he'd received when his father had died and had borrowed more from the bank, but it had been worth every penny. In five years he'd already managed to pay back the loan and had started to recoup his own money.

Then, of course, he had his family. His mom had been ten years younger than his pop. She was closing in on retirement age, but she refused to slow down — even for a second. She still worked as a receptionist in the small hospital on the outskirts of town. She often called in on her way home from work for a coffee and a chat. James would sit and listen to the gossip that she'd picked up from the hospital, unable to believe what some of the doctors and nurses got up to.

James' father had been the town's one and only medical examiner, right up until the final stroke that had taken his life over five years ago. He still missed his pop. He'd been a vibrant man with a real zest for life. He'd always had a smile on his face and a spring in his step. James' mom always said how alike he and his dad were, but James wasn't so sure. He hadn't felt that full of vitality in a long time.

James had two pain-in-the-ass sisters who had blessed him with the cutest niece and nephew. It had been several months since he'd seen his youngest sister, but she lived a few hours away and they didn't get together as often as James would like. Lucy had a four-year-old boy called Justin who was the spitting image of his mother, and she was currently six months pregnant with their second child. James would have liked to spend as much time with his nephew as he did with Hope, but there wasn't a lot they could do about it. Will's job as a wildlife biologist was down in the John Twain National Forest. It was a specialised job and something he couldn't do living in Providence.

He was grateful for his niece and nephew, especially as he wasn't likely to ever have children of his own. It wasn't that he didn't like children or didn't want any, but being gay and living in a small town around small-minded people wasn't conducive to having any. The only other gay men he knew in town were in the closet, just like him. And he only knew about those because he'd seen them in a gay bar he'd visited in St Louis. It was a couple of hours from Providence, but was the closest gay friendly place James knew of near their little town.

Being gay in a small town like Providence could be a lonely existence, but James didn't have any idea how to change it, or even if he wanted to. He didn't want to move, but he was starting to believe there was no alternative if he didn't want to be alone for the rest of his life. But he couldn't think about that. He had a lot in his life to be thankful for.

Time to stop feeling sorry for yourself, James. Suck it up.

Anthony caught his attention and pushed the dessert through the hatch in the wall.

"Here you go, beautiful." James placed the large dessert in front of his niece. "One triple chocolate fudge sundae with marshmallows and chocolate sprinkles."

He leaned in conspiratorially near Hope's ear and whispered, keeping his voice quiet, but loud enough for his sister to overhear, "I made sure there are extra sprinkles."

James found himself on the winning end of a wide, toothless grin. "Thank you, Uncle James!"

James grinned and ruffled the kid's hair. She was the cutest damn five-year-old he'd ever seen, but then he was biased. "Don't forget to share it with your mom, okay?"

Hope nodded enthusiastically and tucked in. "Okay!"

James didn't think his sister would be getting much dessert. She rolled her eyes when Hope missed her mouth and spilled chocolate down her top, but her lips were curved up into a smirk.

"So, what's up, sis?" James took a seat next to his sister and nudged her shoulder. "I haven't seen you in over a week. You been busy?"

Maria nodded. "This damn dissertation is kicking my ass."

Hope gasped. "You swore, Mommy!"

James bit back a grin. They had to be careful what they said with little ears around now. They hadn't had to worry when Hope was a baby, but she was five now and took in everything she heard.

"I know." Maria nodded. "I'm a very bad mommy. You shouldn't listen to a word I say, okay?"

Hope gave a wide-eyed nod and took another bite of chocolate fudge. When James met his sister's gaze, she was grinning mischievously and he couldn't help but match her expression.

"I've got a d-a-t-e on Saturday night," Maria said, remembering to spell out the word so that Hope wouldn't understand.

"Yeah, with who?" James asked.

"John Delucca."

James cocked his head to the side and pursed his lips. "Is that the kid that used to follow you home from school when you were in eighth grade?"

"Yep, that's John. He's a dentist now, got his own practice."

"You looking to get some work done?"

"Ha ha."

"I thought you didn't like him."

Maria rolled her eyes. "We were *thirteen*. I didn't like any boys back then... Well, except Jason Priestley. I would have made an exception for him."

James chuckled. "You and me both."

"Speaking of, what's going on with *your* love life, brother dearest?"

James snagged his sister's spoon and took a large bite of Hope's sundae. "Mmm...that should be illegal," he said moaning loudly. Hope giggled.

"Answer the question, James."

"What? You honestly expect me to have a love life here? Get a grip."

"We're not in Kansas anymore, Toto."

James rolled his eyes. "No, we're in butt crack Missouri. Not a whole hell of a lot of difference from where I'm standing." James winced at his language and looked at Hope, but she was digging out marshmallows from the bottom of her sundae glass and didn't appear to have heard.

"You always were a glass half empty kind of guy."

"And you always were a pain in the..." James caught himself just in time. Hope was looking at them again, her head swivelling back and forth between them both, hanging on every word. "Neck."

Maria took back her spoon and scooped out some chocolate. "You know, if you'd just tell Mom already, she'd have you set up with someone before the week is out."

"Stay out of it, Maria," James warned.

"Look, I'm just saying, if you told her, she—"

"It's none of your business. Now—please drop it."

Maria threw her napkin on the table. "I don't get you sometimes. Why the hell won't you tell her? Mom loves you, the same way she loves all of us. Do you honestly believe she'd think any less of you? In fact, I'm sure she already knows. She—"

James glared at his sister. "Have you said anything?"

"No, but she's not stupid. She's an intelligent woman and you are a thirty-year-old man that's—what? *Never* had a girlfriend? The woman gave birth to you. She knows you better than anyone. Trust me—she knows you're gay!"

Maria's last sentence had been loud. James looked over his shoulder to the old couple sitting in the corner, but they were immersed in their own conversation and didn't look as though they'd heard.

"Christ, can you keep it down?" James fumed.

"What's gay?" Hope asked James.

"Perfect, just perfect. You want to explain that, genius?" James scowled at his sister.

Maria didn't miss a beat.

"It means Uncle James is happy, pumpkin," she said, scooping a spoonful of ice cream out of the glass. "Especially when he plays with men."

Well. That was one way to explain it. Still, she wasn't wrong.

"Doesn't he like to play with girls?" Hope asked.

"No, darling. He thinks girls are silly."

Hope giggled then went back to her chocolate.

"So is Mom coming round tonight?"

"Jesus, Maria, you don't give up, do you?"

"Hey—" Maria lifted both hands out in front of her. "I wasn't even talking about that. I need to ask her to babysit Friday night."

James relaxed his shoulders and nodded. "As far as I know, yeah. She still calls in most nights before she goes home."

"I think she's lonely. And she's working herself into the ground at that damn hospital."

"I think it's *because* she's lonely that she does work so hard. The more hours she works, the less time she has to spend in an empty house."

Maria nodded. "Sure, I can understand that, but it's not doing her any good. She needs to get out and meet people, but she's not interested. I keep giving her brochures for local events and clubs she could join, but she won't even give them a go."

"It's got to be hard for her to go on her own," James reasoned. "Maybe if you went with her the first couple of times, until she met people, she might feel better about going."

"Who's going to watch Hope?" Maria frowned. "I suppose I can get Laurie to look after her, but…"

"What am I, chopped liver?"

"You'd look after Hope?" Maria stared at him, open-mouthed. "For the entire night?"

"Uh, let me just check my hectic schedule. Yeah, for the whole night. Idiot."

Maria was already shaking her head. "I don't know. She can be a handful. You'll probably end up regretting it."

James grinned. "You kidding me? We'll have fun, won't we, Hope?"

Hope's eyes lit up. "Can we have a tea party with cake?"

"Of course. I'll bring the cake and you can make the tea," James bargained.

Maria chuckled. "Now this I've got to see."

Just over an hour after Maria and Hope left the diner, James' mother Gladys came in and took her usual seat in a booth near the back. James was busy serving a couple of young women who worked at the mall. They tossed their hair and batted their eyelashes at him every time they came in, but James didn't mind. He played along for the most part, as he did with all the women who came in to eat, and just hoped they never asked him out. It would only make both parties uncomfortable when he turned them down.

"So how was work today, ladies?" he asked, placing two slices of peach and pecan pie in front of them.

Jane, the bottle blonde who was the more outspoken of the two, smiled suggestively. "It was busy. Brittany and I were thinking about going out for a drink tonight, weren't we, Brit?"

Brittany nodded her agreement and Jane ploughed on. "We're in need of a little...*stress* relief."

That was James' cue. "Well, I'm sure you'll have fun. Enjoy your pie. Excuse me." With a small smile and a quick nod of his head he made a hasty retreat, but he noticed the frown on Jane's lips before she schooled her features. He made his mother a cup of cappuccino and joined her in the booth.

"Who are they?" his mom asked, nodding at the women.

James instinctually turned his head and caught Jane staring at him. He looked away quickly. "Just a couple of shop assistants from the mall. They're in here a few times a week."

"Hmm, well, I wouldn't encourage them if I were you or you'll never see the back of them. Unless you meant to encourage them?" His mom's face was filled with something that looked like hope, which pretty much put to rest Maria's claim that his mom already knew about his sexuality. Either she didn't know or she was a damn good actress.

"I wasn't encouraging them," he replied. "I was being friendly. Anyway, how was your day, Mom?"

Gladys rolled her eyes. "Manic as usual. I didn't sit down all day."

James stirred his coffee then pointed the spoon at his mother and narrowed his eyes. "You work too hard. It's time you slowed down."

"Pfft! I'm not on my deathbed yet, you know. Plenty of life left in this old dog."

"You've worked your whole life. Why don't you think about retiring soon? Wouldn't you prefer to spend your time doing something fun?"

Gladys rolled her eyes. "Work *is* fun. Well…sometimes."

James was about to explain the difference between work and fun, but he thought better of it. That was an argument he never won. And he really didn't want to put his mother in a bad mood. His sister would be calling later to ask Mom to babysit and he'd never hear the end of it if she was short-tempered because of him. Besides, what the hell did he know? Work was all he did too, wasn't it? James couldn't remember the last time he had gone out and had some fun.

"So what's the gossip from the hospital today?" He made the decision to move the conversation onto safer ground and it worked.

Gladys' face lit up. She really did love that damn hospital — there was no question about it. "You remember I told you about Nurse Maxine and Dr Butler?"

James pursed his lips and scrunched his eyebrows together, trying to remember the names and what his mother had said about them. "Are those the two that have been having an affair?"

Gladys made a tutting noise. "No. That's Kristy and Dr Jenkins. Nurse Maxine and Dr Butler are the two whose husbands have been having an affair, with each other."

James nearly choked on his coffee. "You never told me that!"

"Didn't I? I could have sworn I did." His mom looked thoughtful.

James was absolutely certain she hadn't told him. *That* was something he would most definitely have remembered. He could count the number of gay people he knew in Providence on the fingers of one hand, and whenever the residents in town got wind of a story like that it was all they talked about for months. And, even when they stopped talking about it, they never forgot it.

James didn't like to get involved in the gossip around town, but he'd heard about a teacher from the high school who had lost his job when the board had found out he was gay. Of course, they hadn't come right out and fired him for that reason, because he would have sued, but it had been too much of a coincidence to have been for anything else. Mr Keller had taught art at the school for over fifteen years—he'd taught James, in fact—then three weeks after his neighbour saw him kiss his partner goodbye, it was goodbye job. Apparently the cutback had been 'planned all along'.

That was the way it worked in Providence. People would stab you in the back as soon as look at you. The prejudice wasn't always out in the open, but just because it couldn't always be seen didn't mean it wasn't there. James had heard that Mr Keller hadn't been able to find a job since losing his position at the school and was considering moving out of state, even though he'd grown up in Providence and didn't want to have to leave.

"No, you definitely didn't tell me that," James told his mother.

Gladys shrugged. "Not much to tell, really. It's been going on for months apparently, but their wives only found out about it a couple of weeks ago. Dr Butler came in and told everyone at the hospital what her husband had been up to."

"Where does her husband work?"

"He's a paramedic."

"Wow, so he's at the hospital too?"

Gladys nodded. "They both are. Maxine's husband is a radiologist."

"Jesus, that must have been pretty uncomfortable for everyone involved."

"It was. Today the situation reached boiling point when all four of them argued in the corridor in front of the staff. There were patients and relatives around, too."

James leant forward in his seat. "So what happened?"

"A lot of shouting and screaming mainly. John—the radiologist—told his wife he's leaving her, but Dr Butler's husband, Derrick, said he wouldn't even consider leaving his wife and she's sticking by him. If you ask me, *she* should leave *him*. Why would any woman want to be married to a gay man? She probably thinks she can change him, or that he isn't really gay, he was just experimenting. Tempted to the dark side." Gladys snorted. "Fool."

James felt his cheeks fill with heat. He really wanted to change the subject. He felt embarrassed talking about such issues with his mom and it was too damn close to home for his liking. Why he couldn't tell his mother about his own sexuality, he wasn't sure. Deep down he supposed he hoped Maria was right—that his mom already knew about his sexuality—but that wasn't why he hadn't said anything. The main reason was because he had a good relationship with his mom and he didn't want that to change—not that he knew for sure it would, but he didn't want to take the chance. It didn't matter anyway. It wasn't as if James were seeing anyone of importance. If that changed, then he might reconsider telling her.

You sure about that, James?

"So anything else happen at work today?" Just as he asked the question the bell above the diner door chimed. James looked over his shoulder to see who had entered and groaned. Mrs McCormick was staring at James' mother, her face twisted into its usual scowl. She caught James' eye and turned the glare on him before whispering conspiratorially in her twin sister's ear.

Mrs Peters was not nearly as caustic as her sister, who had a tongue as sharp as a Samurai sword. Quite the opposite in fact — May was a pleasure to be around and the one person who had the ability to silence Mrs McCormick with just a glance. But that particular ability didn't look as though it was working today. Mrs McCormick definitely had a bee in her bonnet about something. James groaned inwardly. What the hell did the old battle-axe want with him today?

The sisters rarely came in to eat, rather just to moan about one thing or another. Last week James' new sidewalk sign had been an eyesore and an accident waiting to happen. The week before it had been the poor condition of the sidewalk — like that was his damn fault. But it didn't seem to matter if James was at fault or not — as far as Betty McCormick was concerned, James was always to blame.

"Yes, actually," James' mom continued, completely ignoring the bell, Mrs McCormick and her sister. The sisters were the same age as James' mother, but that was where the similarity between the twins ended. From what James had been able to understand of the situation, they'd never got along. James didn't know why, but he'd bet his bottom dollar there was a story in there somewhere. "I guess you could say something else happened. I saw someone today I haven't seen in quite a while — years, in fact. You'd remember him too, no doubt. You two used to spend a lot of time together."

"Yeah? Who's that?" Distractedly, James held his finger up to Mrs McCormick, indicating he'd be along in a minute, then turned his attention back to his mother.

"Hank Jacobs' son, Matt," Gladys said. She spared a moment to shoot a glare at the sisters, which under different circumstances might have made James smile. But he couldn't force out a smile after his mother's revelation. He could barely breathe.

His stomach lurched violently at the mention of the name that had haunted his dreams since high school. He'd thought about Matt too many times to count over the last ten years, had never stopped thinking about him, in fact. Matt had been the biggest mistake James had ever made… or never made, as the case might be. For as long as he lived he would regret the things he'd said to Matt and what he'd done to him in the last week of high school. James had always wondered if he'd get a chance to tell Matt how sorry he was. If there was a way to take it all back, to make things right between them again, he'd do it in a heartbeat. But he thought it might be too late to make amends. Too much time had passed and he doubted Matt would ever forgive him for what he'd done.

"Yeah." When James finally found his voice it was shaky and sounded distant as though it were coming from someone else. "Of course I remember Matt. He was my best friend in high school."

His mother nodded. "I remember."

"What was he doing at the hospital?"

"His father just passed away."

James sighed heavily and the knot in his stomach tightened. "Oh. I'm sorry to hear that. Did you talk to him?"

"For a few minutes, yes. He was collecting his father's effects."

James' mouth was suddenly as dry as a damn desert. "What did he say?"

"Not much." Gladys shrugged. "He seemed a bit shell-shocked, which is understandable, of course. We mostly just passed the time of day and I offered my condolences. I told him to let me know if he needs anything. Planning a funeral is not one of the easiest things to do and I don't think he has any help. Hank was the last to go of his brothers and there's no one left on his mother's side."

"Did Matt say if he's going to be sticking around town for a while?"

"He didn't say, but it will be at least a week until he gets a date for the funeral, I'd imagine. Maybe more."

"Do you know where he's staying?" James couldn't look his mom in the eye. He didn't want her to see how important the answers to his questions were, because that would lead to questions of her own and James couldn't answer them. "I'd like to pay my condolences."

Gladys shook her head. "No, but I can't see him staying at a hotel when his old house is empty. I'd imagine he'd stay there. Didn't they live out near the river?"

James' heart started beating faster just at the mention of the place they'd spent most of their time when they were in high school. It was the last place he'd ever spoken to Matt, too. It held a lot of good memories for James, but also the worst of them. "Yeah, yeah, they did."

"I'm sure he'd appreciate you calling by to pay your respects."

Matt was more likely to punch James on sight than appreciate him calling by his house, and rightly so. But James couldn't let the opportunity pass without going to see Matt to tell him how sorry he was, both about his father passing and for what he'd done to Matt when they were eighteen. James' mother didn't know what had happened between them. Maria was the only person James had confided in. As far as his mom and everyone else knew, James and Matt had simply not stayed in touch when they'd gone to their respective colleges.

If only that were the case.

"You'd better see what Betty wants." Gladys nodded towards Mrs McCormick at the counter. "If looks could kill, you'd be dead already. And that long-suffering sister of hers looks about ready to drop."

Sure enough, when James looked over his shoulder he discovered his mom hadn't been exaggerating. May didn't look well at all. James rushed over and put a hand on her shoulder.

"Mrs Peters, come and sit down." James started to lead the old woman to a booth seat at the back of the diner, but

Mrs McCormick batted his hand away and grabbed hold of her sister's arm.

"I'm perfectly capable of looking after my own sister, young man."

James would have rolled his eyes if he thought he could get away with it, but Betty McCormick didn't miss a trick and James wasn't that brave.

"Of course," he replied. "May, let me get you a glass of water."

"Thank you," Betty replied curtly.

"Thank you," May echoed. Her voice was quieter than usual and contained none of her usual cheer.

"Do you want to see a doctor?" James asked. "I could call an ambulance."

Mrs McCormick scowled at James. "She doesn't need a doctor," she said, shooing James away. "She just needs to sit down for a few minutes."

Much to Betty's obvious chagrin, James ignored her and addressed her sister. "Mrs Peters?"

May shook her head and offered James a small smile. "No, thank you, dear, I just need to rest my bones and I'll be right as rain in no time. I won't say no to that glass of water, though—with ice, if you have some."

"Coming right up." James nodded and left to prepare the drink. Betty was fussing over her sister when James slipped into the kitchen to get ice. He put a couple of cubes in the glass and was making his way back into the diner when the chef, Anthony, caught his attention.

"Everything all right, boss?" Anthony was slicing lemons with a precision that never failed to amaze James. The chef had been with him since he'd opened the diner and was an incredible cook. He wasn't ashamed to admit he'd be lost without him.

"Mrs McCormick," James said by way of explanation.

Anthony chuckled. "Say no more. I'll check on you in five minutes and, if you look to be in trouble, I'll invent some disaster in the kitchen."

James raised his hand in a salute. "Much obliged."

He carried the water back into the diner and handed the glass to Mrs Peters. "Here you go, drink this."

May took hold of the glass and took a small sip. "Ah, that's lovely," she said around a sigh before placing the glass down on the table. "Thank you."

"It's no trouble," James replied. "Are you sure you wouldn't like me to call someone?"

May shook her head. "No, I'm okay now. Just one of my turns. I think I overexerted myself, that's all. I need to remember that I can't do the things I used to."

Mrs McCormick snorted. "You do twice as much now as you did when you were younger and there's still a lot of years left in you yet."

May grinned and the impish expression took years off her face. "You'd have to say that, being my twin," she replied. "But we both know we're not as young as we once were."

"So what can I do for you today, ladies?" James asked. "Can I get you something to eat?"

The concern that had been present on Mrs McCormick's face a moment before disappeared to be replaced by her usual scowl. "We didn't come here for food," she answered shortly. "We're here on serious business."

James suppressed a smile. He'd just bet they were. "Oh? What is it I can do for you, Mrs McCormick?"

"I have a complaint. Last night was the neighbourhood watch municipal court meeting and you were absent for the second month running. What do you have to say for yourself?"

Crap, was what he wanted to say. Betty's cold, hard stare made James feel like he was on trial. He gave an involuntary shiver.

"I'm sorry I couldn't make the meeting last night, but one of my staff called in sick and I had to stay on. By the time I found cover, the meeting was nearly over and it wasn't worth attending, but I knew you ladies would fill me in on the details." James offered his most apologetic smile and hoped like hell Betty fell for it. The truth was he'd completely forgotten about the meeting, but there was no way in hell he'd admit that to Betty McCormick. She'd have him hung, drawn and quartered. He just hoped lying to a little old lady wasn't the type of offence that would see him sent straight to hell without passing go.

Betty narrowed her eyes, but she didn't ask James which of his staff had been ill. *Thank God*—he hadn't thought that far in advance when he'd made up the lie on the spot.

"The meeting was…enlightening," Betty said.

James doubted that very much. "If you'd just let me get a coffee, I'll join you ladies in a minute. Can I get you anything to drink?"

"No, thank you," Betty replied curtly.

"May?" James enquired, "Would you like anything else?"

May already looked a damn sight better than she had earlier and the faint blush that appeared on her cheeks made her seem even more so. "I wouldn't mind a slice of that wonderful peach pie," she said quietly.

James' grin got bigger when he saw Betty scowl at her sister.

"Absolutely," he replied. "And, for you, I'll make it an extra big slice."

Chapter Two

Matt's gaze alternated between the key in his hand and the familiar house he hadn't seen in over two years. He doubted his father would have bothered to change the locks after he had left, but that wasn't the reason he still sat in his car, staring at the house in which he'd grown up. He was being a big ole chicken-shit, pure and simple. He was afraid to go in the house, afraid of what it would do to his carefully constructed composure. He'd been holding it together pretty well since he'd found out about his father's death earlier that day. He'd been on autopilot at the hospital, signing the forms and collecting his father's belongings. It had been easier than he'd expected. But, of course, the real test had come when he'd had to go in and see his father. That had almost broken through his defences. Almost, but not quite. Over the years he'd become adept at schooling his emotions and burying them deep down inside where they couldn't hurt him.

His pop had looked peaceful lying in bed, younger even than when Matt had last seen him. He'd wondered absently if his father had looked that way in the years since Matt had been gone or if it was something that came only with death. Matt's father hadn't been the same man since he'd lost his wife. Lilly had died several years before her husband, when Matt had been a teenager. He had to wonder if the smile on his pop's face was because they were at last together again. Matt certainly hoped such a thing was possible.

Looking at his father's peaceful face, he could have been fooled into thinking he was simply sleeping, but when Matt had touched his hand and trailed his fingers over his father's knuckles there had been no denying he was touching the skin of a person whose soul no longer inhabited their body. His hand had been cold — unusually so. It felt wrong, unnatural. He was colder to the touch than marble.

Matt had wanted to shout at his father, to ask him what the hell he was playing at. He wanted to know why he had to die and leave Matt all alone in the world. Why? He just wanted to know why. But as he'd stood at the bedside, looking down at the man who'd had a hand in shaping the person Matt had become, he knew it was pointless to wish for such things. His father would never be able to tell him anything again. It didn't matter how much Matt wished otherwise.

He took a last look at the key in his hand and took off his seatbelt. He couldn't sit in the damn car all night. He'd been in such a rush to get to the hospital, he hadn't even considered coming home first to drop off his belongings. He didn't want to go in now, but he knew he couldn't keep putting it off.

When he'd got out of the car, he retrieved his suitcase from the trunk. It was only when he had the case in his hand that he remembered the whisky he'd thrown in almost as an afterthought. It was just what he needed to settle his damn nerves. He walked the familiar path up to the front door, slid the key into the lock and turned it. The door opened with a welcoming creak.

Matt didn't bother looking around the house. He went straight upstairs to his old room, pushed open the door and switched on the light. His bedroom looked exactly as he'd left it two years ago. Actually, it hadn't changed much since he was a teenager. Matt wasn't sure why, but the fact that his pop hadn't touched the room since he'd left made him sad. It was like his father had been waiting for him to come home. *Don't think about it. Think happy thoughts.* But Matt didn't know if he had a happy thought left in his head. None came to him.

He swallowed down a lump in his throat and emptied the

contents of his case on the bed. He hung most of his clothes in the small closet and stuffed everything else in the chest of drawers near the window. He left the whisky on the nightstand — ready and waiting for him to drink himself into oblivion. Then he'd get up, ignore the hangover and start making arrangements for the funeral. It wasn't something he was looking forward to, but it had to be done. When he'd finished putting everything away he took a moment to look around his old room. It smelt musty, as though it hadn't seen any fresh air in a long time, so Matt crossed the room, pulled back the drapes and opened the window.

It was a midsummer evening and there wasn't a lot of fresh air to be had, but the slight breeze that found its way into the room did help to alleviate some of the stuffiness. Matt went downstairs and took a look around the living room. As with his bedroom, nothing in the room had been altered. His pop hadn't so much as put a fresh coat of paint on the walls or replaced the throws on the old sofa. On the wall above the fireplace sat a picture of Matt in high school. He didn't think about that last year in school very often. Mostly the year had gone by without event. But the last week before graduation had sullied the entire school year for Matt. It had become all he could remember about high school, about his friends, about his life here in Providence. He'd tried hard to forget the day that had changed everything, but it was always there in the back of his mind, taunting him, never allowing him to be truly happy.

And the rest of his childhood *had* been happy. He'd had parents who loved him, he'd been popular in school. He'd had a good life. But it had been a long time since he'd felt content — at peace with himself and with the world at large. His house had always been filled with love and laughter. He hadn't realised how much he missed those times until he saw the smile in his fourteen-year-old eyes. It had been a long time since a smile had made it all the way to his eyes.

Matt tore his gaze away from the picture and headed to the kitchen when his emotions threatened to overwhelm him. It, like every other room in the house, was exactly as it had been when he'd left. Nothing had been touched. Matt crossed to the cabinet above the sink and retrieved two tumblers. One he filled with water and the other he left empty for the whisky.

After he'd made sure all the doors and windows were secure, Matt carried the glasses to his room. He poured out a generous amount of whisky and added a little of the water. He took a sip and grimaced. He'd never liked the taste of whisky particularly, but you didn't have to like it to drink it, did you? Matt took another look around. There was still one room in the house he hadn't had the guts to enter – his pop's bedroom. He couldn't think why that room would be any different to the others in the house. He supposed that room seemed more personal. It wasn't a shared space – just his father's. It would smell like him, feel like him. It would remind Matt of the mistakes he'd made, of the argument he'd had with his father, and he didn't want to think about that just yet. He couldn't.

He threw back the rest of the whisky in the glass and poured another, downing it quicker than the first. *Don't be such a coward. It's only a room. You've been it in countless times in the past. This time won't be any different.* Only it would be different. Everything was different now. After another couple of drinks to psych himself up, Matt put down the glass and crossed the hall until he stood outside his pop's bedroom. He took a deep breath. *You can do this.* Slowly, he pushed open the door.

His pop's room was the same as he remembered and, just as Matt had suspected, it smelt like his pop, too. A mixture of laundry detergent and that God-awful cheap cologne he insisted on wearing, even though Matt had bought him more expensive brands over the years in the hope he'd throw the old stuff away.

Matt crossed the space and sat down on his father's bed. He'd expected the bed to be unmade, but it wasn't. The sheets were clean and it was neat and tidy. He'd never known his pop to make his bed when he left it. A cold shiver ran the length of his spine. Had his pop somehow known what was going to happen to him when he'd got up that morning? Had he suspected his time was at an end, even subconsciously? Matt picked up a pillow and held it to his nose. It smelt mostly of detergent, but his pop's scent still clung to the material. Matt tried to swallow down the lump that had formed in the back of his throat, but felt the sting of tears behind his eyes.

"Stubborn old bastard. What the hell did you have to go and die for, huh?"

Matt fell back onto the bed and hugged the pillow to his chest, letting the tears fall freely from his eyes. He cried and cried and just when he thought he had no tears left he cried some more. Soon the tears morphed into hiccups then dry, heaving sobs that wouldn't abate. When the tears finally dried up, Matt supposed he should go back to his own bedroom, but he didn't have the energy or inclination to move. With a sigh, he closed his eyes and, though his mind was in overdrive, filled with unwelcome thoughts and images, he eventually fell asleep.

* * * *

The sun was beaming in through the gap in the drapes and warming the left side of his face when Matt woke up. His mouth tasted like crap and he had the headache from hell. He cracked open his eyes and turned to gaze around the room. He was startled at first to realise he wasn't lying in his own bed, but still in his father's room. When the events of the previous night came back to him Matt sighed heavily and got off the bed. He hadn't even changed before he'd crashed out the night before and he was in desperate need of a shower.

The water must have been on a timer because it was deliciously hot when Matt stepped under the spray. It soothed some of the tension out of his muscles and went some way to making him feel human again. As soon as he'd got himself dressed, he put on a pot of coffee and rummaged around in the cupboards to see if there was anything edible. His pop had never been much of a cook, but Matt suspected there would be bread at the very least, maybe eggs. Surprisingly, he was all out of luck. Apart from condiments and a few tins of soup, the cupboards were empty. What had his father been living on? If he intended to stay in town for anything longer than a day or two then he'd need to buy some groceries to see him through to the end of the week. It was a given he'd be around at least that amount of time while he arranged his pop's funeral, which was something he didn't want to have to think about but couldn't be put off.

He sat down at the kitchen table to drink his coffee. It wasn't particularly good coffee, but Matt had never considered himself a coffee snob. As long as it was hot, sweet and black then he was good to go. While he drank, Matt made a mental list of the things he had to do. The first and most important thing was to call the funeral directors. That was something that really couldn't wait. He hoped they would be able to advise him of the other things that needed to be done, because Matt didn't have a clue where to start. The bank would have to be informed of his pop's death too, he supposed, as would his father's lawyer, Larry Thorne.

Matt had some money saved that he could use to pay for the funeral if he had to, but he was sure his father had been paying into some sort of life insurance policy that would help with costs. Larry would know more about that. Matt couldn't believe he had to think about such things. He never thought he'd see this day. Parents were supposed to be invincible, weren't they? Always there for you. But Matt knew from experience that wasn't the case. He'd lost his mom to cancer almost twelve years ago and that had been one of the hardest things he'd lived through. But he'd had someone to help him through then, and although it had been a difficult time, it had been made easier by having people who cared about him stand at his side and give him support. One person in particular had been there for Matt when he was sixteen. He'd thought they would always be friends, but he'd been wrong.

Matt scrubbed a hand over his face while he tried to think about what to do next. He hoped he hadn't forgotten anything. He didn't know what he was doing, but there was no one around he could ask for help. A sudden wave of loneliness crashed over him, but he did his best to put it out of his mind. It wasn't the time to throw himself a pity party. He had things to do for his dad. Maybe Matt could think about falling apart after his pop had been put to rest. Until then, he had to hold it together.

The first thing he needed to do was eat breakfast. He wasn't especially hungry, but he knew he would function better when he had a decent meal inside him. Coffee and fresh air weren't going to cut it this time, and so Matt grabbed his car keys and headed out of the door.

It wasn't even nine, but already the sun was hot, baking Matt's skin as soon as he stepped outside. The air-conditioning system in his car only worked when it felt like it and it seemed today was one of the days it had decided it didn't want to do anything that even closely resembled work. Matt groaned and rolled down the windows, but the gust of warm air that whipped past his face did nothing to help cool him down. Christ, Matt had forgotten how hot the summers got in Missouri. It hadn't been this hot in Des Moines — at least it hadn't felt like it.

It had taken Matt over six hours to drive home to Providence and the more miles he'd covered, the less he'd wanted to go back to Iowa. What did he have there waiting for him anyway? He wasn't leaving behind anything of any importance. He might have stayed for Tom, before the man had shown his true colours. If he were being honest with himself, even on the first day they'd met, he'd known that it was never going to be anything more than casual between them. Tom might not have come out and told him that in so many words, but it had been evident in his actions. There had never been any doubt in Matt's mind that Tom was gay, however he was so firmly entrenched in the closet, Matt doubted he would ever find the courage he would need to step out and take ownership of who he was. To admit it to the world, he would first need to admit it to himself. Maybe he'd be ready one day, though Matt would be a fool to wait around for him to do so.

If he discounted Tom then there was nothing else that Matt would be leaving behind. He'd quit his job and his cat had deserted him. He had the house, but it wouldn't be too difficult to put it on the market and he didn't have many possessions he could call his own. Maybe he could stay in Missouri for a while after the funeral. It was as good a place as any. It was home. Matt would need to find out what the situation was with his father's house first, but that wouldn't be too hard to do. He knew his pop owned the house, had for some years, he just didn't know what would happen to it now that his pop had passed away. Larry would be able to tell him. He'd give him a call when he got back.

The grocery shopping didn't take long. Matt considered stopping off at a diner to get breakfast, but he changed his mind at the last minute. Sweat poured down his face as he drove home. He'd have to take another shower as soon as he got in. Then he remembered a place from his youth. It was somewhere he used to spend a lot of time. He hadn't been there in years, but he'd visited often when he was in high school—nearly every day, in fact. Matt wondered if his spot by the river looked the same as it had back then. Had someone else discovered it? Was someone else calling it theirs now? Before he could change his mind, he took the left turn that led to the woods and parked near the path that led to the river. He looked around and smiled. It all looked pretty much the same as he remembered.

He made his way through the trees, taking the familiar

route he'd walked so many times before. The closer he got to the river, the more his stomach cramped with anticipation. Was it possible for somewhere to be both your favourite *and* most hated place at the same time? After a few moments of walking the narrow path through the trees, Matt stood in the clearing on the edge of the water. The place was exactly as he remembered it, but the familiarity didn't bring the comfort he'd expected it to. He wasn't sure exactly what he'd been hoping to find, but it wasn't there...or rather, *he* wasn't there.

The temperature must have been well into the nineties. As Matt wiped the sweat off his forehead and stared at the inviting water, a small smile played on his lips. When he was in high school Matt would skinny-dip in this river. It was a secluded area that no one ever came to and it had been his sanctuary until the day that had changed everything. Matt didn't let himself think about that day anymore. In the beginning it had been all he had thought about. He'd cursed himself a hundred times over for doing what he'd done and wondered how different his life might have been if he hadn't kissed his best friend, if he hadn't ruined everything.

Matt took another look around the clearing and, when he was satisfied he was alone, he took off his clothes. Completely naked, he waded into the water. Skinny-dipping here at the river was something Matt had done often when he was a teenager and, even though he felt odd at first and worried someone might come by and see, he'd lost all his inhibitions by the time he got in the water. It was cold to begin with, a serious shock to his system, but it felt good against his overheated skin. He floated on his back, gazing up at the cloudless sky, and for a short time it was as though he didn't have a care in the world, as though he were seventeen again and his mother and father were still alive and James was still his best friend. James—who'd had the starring role in every one of his fantasies. James—who had crushed Matt's heart without even realising he'd held it in his hands.

Matt swam for another few minutes then got out of the water. There was a large rock on the riverbank that Matt used to sunbathe on so he took his usual spot, stretched out and closed his eyes, letting the sun dry his body and warm his face. He could almost convince himself he was happy... almost.

"Hello, Matt."

Matt practically jumped out of his skin. His eyes flew open and he raised a hand to his chest, fighting to catch his breath.

"Jesus. You scared the hell out of me." When Matt looked up and put a face to the voice he hadn't heard in over ten years, he froze. Then his eyes became wide with panic and his heart hammered heavily in his chest.

"Relax, Matt, I'm not going to hurt you," James said quietly.

Matt lifted a hand to shield his eyes from the sun, embarrassed by his overreaction to James' presence. "What the hell are *you* doing here anyway?"

James let out a long, slow breath. "I heard you were in town. I'm so sorry about your dad."

When the shock of seeing James finally abated, Matt had the presence of mind to cover his dignity, even if the action was tardy. He edged off the rock and reached for his clothes. "You didn't answer my question. What are you doing here?"

James looked up and met his eyes. "I've been looking for you. I wanted to talk to you."

"What could you possibly have to say to me? Or did you come to start trouble, huh? Is that it? Did you come to hit me again? Show the little faggot how big and strong and macho you are?"

James recoiled at Matt's words as though he'd been physically slapped, and a flicker of emotion that Matt couldn't place passed over his face.

"I came to apologise," he said.

41

"Well, go on then. I'm waiting"

James took a deep breath. "I'm sorry. I'm so sorry. I know it's—"

"Great, you apologised. Now get lost."

James sighed. "I mean it, Matt. I'm sorry for what I said to you that day and I'm sorry for what I did. I should never have hit you."

Matt shrugged like it didn't make one lick of difference to him, but truth was, he'd wanted to hear those words from James' lips since the day it had happened. But now that James was in front of him and saying them, they didn't feel like enough.

"What the hell do you want from me? You want my forgiveness, is that it?"

"No, I—"

"Well, I can't give it. You hurt me, you…"

"It was never my intention to hurt you. I'm sorry about your face, I—"

"I'm not talking about the punch," Matt said. "The nose healed. It was more than that and you know it. I thought we were friends, I never thought you'd do something like that. I trusted you." Matt laughed, but the sound was devoid of humour. "I guess I was an idiot, right?"

"No," James corrected, "I was the idiot. I was scared and I lashed out, in more ways than one."

Matt heaved a heavy sigh. "Look, I know I shouldn't have kissed you, all right? I know it was wrong. I was way out of line, and believe me, I'm sorry for doing it, but you were my best friend. I thought that you more than anyone else would be able to understand me, would be there for me. I counted on you."

James hung his head and his blond bangs fell forward to cover his eyes. "I said a lot of things that day that I regret, and I wish I could take them back, but I can't. I know how much I hurt you and I'm sorry for that." Finally James looked up and met Matt's gaze. "Didn't it ever occur to you why I acted so strongly that day?" James asked.

"Of course it did," Matt scoffed. "Because you're a homophobic asshole."

James snorted. "I guess you would think that, but surely you know what they say about people that protest the loudest."

Matt tilted his head and stared at his old friend for the longest time, trying to work out what he was trying to say. He couldn't possibly be telling Matt what he thought he was, could he?

"Now wait just a damn minute. Are you trying to say that you're…?"

"Gay," James finished. "Yeah, that's exactly what I'm saying."

Matt stared at James open-mouthed. He couldn't believe what he was hearing. James was gay? That selfish fucking son of a bitch. He'd made Matt feel like shit all those years ago, like there was something wrong with him. He'd made him feel dirty and ashamed of himself and that he wasn't good enough—for James or for anyone. And for a long time Matt had believed him. It had taken him years to stop feeling ashamed for something he had no control over. He often wondered how different his life would have turned out if he'd had the support of his best friend. But he hadn't.

He pulled his shirt over his head and glared at James. How could you forgive someone you once trusted for hurting you like that? He wasn't sure he had the forgiveness in him.

"You've said your piece, now I'd like you to leave." Matt couldn't look at James when he spoke. He was afraid looking into those deep-blue eyes would make his determination crumble, and he couldn't let that happen. Matt was in town for his father—he didn't need this shit right now. Didn't James get that? That just went to prove what a selfish asshole he really was.

James swallowed audibly then nodded his head. "Of course." He turned to leave then paused and lifted his hand slowly until it came to rest on Matt's shoulder. Matt wanted to shrug it off, but he didn't have the energy or the willpower the action would have taken. He just looked at it—anything to avoid looking James in the eye.

"I didn't only come here to tell you how sorry I am. I came to offer my help. I know how hard it was on you when you lost your mom. I was there for you then and I'd like to be here for you now. I lost my own father a few years ago so I know what you're going through. If you need any help with the arrangements for the funeral, you only need to ask."

This time Matt did shrug James' hand away. "I'm sorry to hear about your father, but I don't need any help, thank you. I'm perfectly capable of handling it on my own."

James' mouth curved up into a small smile that never quite reached his eyes. "How did I know you were going to say that?" James shook his head and walked back towards the road. "But if you change your mind, I still live in town. You can find me at—"

"I won't be trying to find you," Matt interrupted. "You don't need to tell me where, because it's never going to happen, understand? We were friends once, but that was a long time ago and you ruined it. We're never going to be friends again."

James held Matt's gaze for a long moment and there appeared to be a trace of pain in his eyes, or was it sadness? Matt didn't know, but he was sure he saw James swallow down a lump in his throat.

"Take care of yourself, Matt."

Matt watched James walk away until he was out of sight. When he was finally alone again, he sat down heavily on the rock and scrubbed a hand over his face. That had been harder than he'd imagined. He'd often thought about what it would feel like to see James again and what he would say to him. He'd had a whole stupid speech planned out in his mind when he was eighteen, but it seemed the years had watered down the inclination to give James a piece of his mind.

Matt wanted to hate James...but he didn't—he couldn't.

They had been the best of friends once. When they were fifteen, Matt had believed that nothing could have ever come between them. They'd known each other's hopes and dreams, each other's secrets, and they'd kept them faithfully. Matt had thought he'd be able to trust James with the biggest secret of all—that he was gay—but it seemed that secret had been too big for James to bear. He hadn't known how to deal with it. He'd lashed out. Of course, now, Matt knew the reason why. James must have been terrified that his own secret would have been revealed, that Matt would have found out they were more alike than he'd realised. What a damn coward James had been. Matt had thought he'd been weak, certainly weaker than his friend, but he'd been wrong. James had been the weak one.

They'd just finished their last year of high school and would be going off to separate colleges when it happened. James had been worried they'd lose touch when they left town and went their separate ways, and Matt had shared in that fear, but what James didn't know was that Matt's reasons had been slightly different to his. A week before they were due to leave, they had come to their place by the river. It had been a beautiful summer's day, hot and sticky—there hadn't been much air. To cool off they'd gone skinny-dipping in the river and were drying out side by side on the rock. James had cracked some stupid joke about Mrs Abraham from the grocery store, and Matt had laughed and laughed until he was doubled over, clutching his sides and gasping for breath. When he'd finally recovered, he'd turned to James, seen the sparkle in his eyes and, in a moment of utter madness, he'd closed the distance between them and kissed his best friend.

It had been an incredibly stupid, impulsive thing to do. He hadn't thought about the consequences. He hadn't taken the time to consider what it would do to their relationship or how it would change things between them. He hadn't thought about anything at all. He'd just done it. He'd leant forward and touched their lips together in the biggest mistake of his life.

At first Matt had thought James was kissing him back, and it had made him happier than he could ever remember being. Matt's heart had raced in his chest when their lips had pressed together more firmly and adrenaline had rushed through his body, filling his dick until it had become harder than it had ever been. He hadn't been able to stop the moan that had escaped his lips, or holding James' head to deepen the kiss. When he'd slipped his tongue inside James' mouth, it had been then that James had pulled back, his mouth open wide with shock, and the reality of the situation had set in. James' face had been clouded with anger and before Matt had been able to do anything to stop it or even raise a hand to protect himself, James had punched him.

It had hurt like hell and while he'd held his head back, trying to stem the flow of blood from his nose, James had jumped up and had started pulling on his clothes, all the while shouting at Matt, enraged. He'd said things Matt had never expected to leave his best friend's lips.

"Stay away from me, freak! You're a faggot. Don't touch me. If you come near me again I'll tell everyone what you tried to do to me..."

There had been more—a barrage of words and insults and accusations that had cut Matt to the core. Had changed him, made him wary of opening up to anyone again.

He'd gone home that day and cried and cried, heartbroken over what he'd done and the things James had said. It turned out his nose had been broken, but the pain in his chest had hurt far worse than the pain in his face. Just as James had demanded, Matt hadn't gone near him again, and a week later they had both gone off to their respective colleges.

Matt had thought about tracking James down in college to apologise for what he'd done, but he never had. He'd been afraid he'd provoke James more. In truth, Matt had been a coward. He couldn't have faced seeing James again, couldn't have stood to see the repulsion in his eyes, so he'd stayed away, but the guilt had eaten him up inside. And every time he'd thought about that day it had reminded him of what James thought he was—a dirty queer that had come on to his straight best friend.

Of course, in time he'd come to realise that he wasn't dirty. There wasn't something wrong with him. He was just different. But it had taken time, years in fact, before he'd made peace with himself. He'd been afraid to even look at a guy in college in case they treated him the same way James had. He hadn't wanted to be laughed at or hurt, not that anyone could have hurt him more than James.

After college he'd started an internship in Iowa and discovered there were other gay men working in the office. That was about the time he had started to feel comfortable in his own skin. But for ten years, while he'd got on with his life and had tried to forget about his best friend and carve out a life for himself, James had never been far from his thoughts. He had often wondered where James was living and what he was doing with his life. Was he married? Did he have children? Did he ever think about Matt? He shouldn't have wanted to know those things about the person who had hurt him so much—he shouldn't have cared, but he had. He did.

Matt supposed he had his answers now, finally. It seemed James was still living in Providence. And he was gay. Was he single? Matt shook the treacherous thought from his head. He was glad he'd never contacted James to apologise for what he'd done, because it seemed James should have been the one to apologise to him. But Matt hadn't seen so much as a whisker of James in ten years, so he couldn't be that sorry for what he'd said and done, could he? What in the hell had he been doing here today?

He'd said he wanted to apologise, but if it was so important to him, why wait ten years? Matt might have fallen out with his father, but the old man knew where he was living. He would have given James his address if he'd asked for it. Besides, the argument with his father had only taken place a couple of years ago. James had had eight whole years to find him before then. So why hadn't he? Because he didn't really care at all. How could he? He was probably just covering himself in case Matt ran into him in town, or heard that he was gay from some other source.

Matt sighed and got up from the rock. It was pointless wondering or asking questions he would never know the answer to. And it worked both ways, he supposed. He'd never sought out James to try to make things right between them, had he?

The best thing he could do would be to forget about James. He needed to put the entire incident behind him and close the book on that chapter of his life. He was in town to deal with his father's funeral arrangements, nothing more. As soon as that was done, he would go back to Des Moines. He might have thought about staying in Providence, but now that he knew James was still in town there was no way he was going to do that. He didn't want to have to see him every day. That would only make things harder. He'd go back to his apartment and find another job just as soon as the funeral was over. It would be for the best. With a renewed sense of purpose, Matt strode back to his car. He had things to do and he couldn't waste any more of his time thinking about James.

* * * *

James took a deep breath and pushed open the diner door. Work was the last place he wanted to be, but his assistant manager, Angela, had told him she could only cover until midday. He might have asked to her to stay, but he knew she had to take her youngest son to the doctor. James couldn't complain about her leaving. He was grateful to her for stepping in at such short notice. She hadn't had to do it. She'd already worked over her hours for the week. She'd been doing him a favour and he wouldn't take advantage.

James hadn't been able to sleep since his mother had told

him Matt was back in town. All he'd been able to think about was finding him and apologising. It was something he should have done many years ago, he knew that, but he'd been a coward and hadn't wanted to see the pain in Matt's eyes when he looked at him. He knew how badly he'd hurt Matt and he'd never forgiven himself for it.

James had hoped seeing Matt again and finally apologising to him would help, but it had only made him feel worse. It wasn't because of the guilt, although that had been as prevalent as always. It was because his stomach had lurched and his breath had caught in his chest when he'd looked at Matt again. After ten long and somewhat lonely years, the attraction was still as strong as it had always been, and even though he had no right to, he couldn't help but wonder if Matt had felt anything when he'd looked at James…well, anything other than the anger and hurt that had been so evident in his eyes.

James had been fifteen the first time he'd looked at Matt as something more than a friend. It had been the first time he'd noticed *any* boy in that way and it had scared the hell out of him. He hadn't wanted to be gay. He hadn't wanted to be different. He and Matt had been playing by the river like they had most days when they got home from school, and had just been in for a swim. The water had been dripping in steady rivulets from Matt's hair down his neck and shoulders and down his smooth, tanned chest. It was the first time he could remember seeing a wet body as something erotic. He'd wanted to move closer and lick the drops away with his tongue. He'd got hard instantly, then he'd become embarrassed.

He'd grabbed his clothes, dressed and got the hell out of there, telling Matt he had to do something for his parents. Of course, that had only been the first time he'd noticed Matt that way. There had been many other times after that, right up until the day Matt had kissed him and he'd panicked and made the worst goddamn mistake of his life. He'd pushed Matt away and punched him and he fucking hated himself for doing that.

James now knew it was stupid, but he'd only freaked out because he'd been naked and he knew Matt would have seen how excited he'd become. They'd been for a swim in the lake and had been drying out on the rock. James remembered saying something to make Matt laugh because he loved the sound of Matt laughing — it was like music to his ears. It had been innocent up until that point, just friends goofing around. To get naked and swim together was something they'd done myriad times before, but it had all changed with that simple, innocent little kiss. The second their lips had touched, James had grown painfully hard like he had that first time he'd reacted to Matt's wet, naked body. And it had reminded him of that first time, too — of the shame he'd felt, of the confusion — and before he could think about what he was doing, he'd pulled away and lashed out.

He could still remember the look Matt had given him. James didn't think it was something he would ever be able to forget. There had been hurt at first and shock undoubtedly — pain even — but it was the disappointment etched into every crevice on Matt's face that had been the hardest to stomach. Matt hadn't believed James would let him down, but that was exactly what he'd gone and done. But he hadn't stopped there, had he? If it had just been the punch there might have been a way back from that.

Bile began to rise in James' throat when he thought about the things he'd said to Matt that day by the lake. He'd been so shocked, so embarrassed, that he'd said things in the heat of the moment that he wished to God he could take back. Not that there was any excuse for the things he'd said. And when he hadn't been able to stand to see the look of disappointment in Matt's eyes anymore, James had turned on his heel and had run away like the coward he was. He'd been too afraid to get in touch with Matt later to apologise, too. He'd been terrified he'd see that look again — the look that had the capacity to break his heart into a thousand little pieces. And the hardest part was that it had been *his* damn fault to begin with. He'd put that look on Matt's face. And what would it have mattered if he'd gone to Matt and he'd had that look on his face anyway? James still saw it every time he closed his eyes. Sometimes, it was all he could see.

He should have found the courage to apologise to Matt before today, he knew that now. He should have got down on his knees and begged Matt to forgive him, begged him not to throw away a friendship that was the most important thing in James' life. He should have admitted everything. After all, what did he have left to lose? He'd already lost the most important thing in his life – Matt's friendship.

But he hadn't apologised and even as he'd said he was sorry earlier by the lake, he'd known it was too little, too late. Matt didn't want anything to do with him, and James couldn't blame his old friend one damn iota.

"Hi, James," Angela greeted brightly when he joined her behind the counter. "How was your morning?"

Pretty fucking awful, was what he wanted to say, but "Good, thanks," was what came out.

"It got real busy after you left, but it calmed down about twenty minutes ago," Angela said, stacking coffee cups on the shelf behind the counter.

James tried to smile at his employee but wasn't sure he managed it. "Thanks for covering for me today, I really appreciate it."

Angela shrugged. "Truth be told, I'm grateful for the extra shifts right now. Lonny's medical care is getting expensive."

Lonny, Angela's son, had a bad case of asthma and was always being admitted to the hospital after a particularly bad attack. But James hadn't known Angela was struggling financially – if she'd have told him, he would have helped.

"Why didn't you say anything? If you needed extra shifts, you know all you had to do was ask. I'll have a look at the rota and see what I can do, and if you need to borrow..."

Angela raised her hand. "I appreciate the offer of extra

51

work, I'll definitely take you up on that, but I'm not a charity case. I don't want to borrow anything. I don't mean to sound ungrateful, I just..."

"You don't. Say no more. I'll give you a call in the morning to let you know what extra shifts I've got going next week, okay?"

Angela smiled brightly. "Yes. Thank you."

James nodded. "Anything else I need to know? No one rang for me while I was away?"

Angela shook her head. "Nope, no messages. Oh, you need more quarters and you're clean out of the peach and pecan pie. Mrs Peters was in earlier with her sister and she polished off the last two pieces."

James smiled. He was glad to hear that. May Peters must be back to full health if she was polishing off two pieces of pie. "That sounds about right. Anthony said he was going to make a fresh batch tomorrow."

"Well then, I guess I'll be going. See you tomorrow afternoon."

"Yeah, tomorrow and I'll give you a call in the morning about those extra shifts, okay?"

"That's great, thanks."

The day was pretty quiet after Angela left to pick up her son. James thought it was going to be another boring and uneventful day until his sister Maria stuck her head in the diner, grinning like the cat that got the cream. When she pushed open the door, her hands were full of shopping bags from the mall.

"Oh Lord, here comes trouble," James quipped. "And here I thought I was in for a quiet afternoon."

Maria rolled her eyes. "You hate quiet afternoons."

"Not always. So what you been up to, dear sister, or do I not want to know the answer to that question?" James cast a wary eye over the array of bags his sister had dumped unceremoniously at her feet. "And where's that gorgeous niece of mine?"

Maria took a seat on one of the stools at the counter and

picked up a menu even though she could probably recite it by heart by now. "To answer your first question, I've been shopping at the mall and I can't remember the last time I had as much fun with my clothes on."

"Maria," James groaned. "Did you have to go there?"

His sister's smile widened. "Oh come on, James. If I can't talk about shopping and sex with my gay brother, who can I talk to about it?"

James checked over his shoulder even though he knew the diner was presently empty. "The shopping I can tolerate, just about," he said. "But come on—you squick me out sometimes with all the sex talk."

"Is that even a word?"

James shrugged. "Don't care. So what's with the marathon shop?"

"I had to pick out a new outfit for my d-a-t-e on Saturday night."

James chuckled when his sister spelled out the word. "You get something nice?"

"Of course!" Maria said as though James had asked the stupidest question ever. "And to answer your second question, the brat is with her father. His Highness is picking her up from school then taking her out for something to eat."

James grinned. "Really? And just how much did you have to pay him to do that?"

Maria's mouth fell open. "I resent that! Just because we're not together anymore doesn't mean John doesn't see his daughter from time to time, you know!"

James waited, eyebrow raised.

"Fine, twenty bucks," Maria admitted. "He said he didn't have any money to buy her dinner. And don't tell Mom, okay?"

"My lips are sealed." Maria's waste of space ex-fiancé— otherwise known as John—was a bone of contention in their family. Fortunately his sister had come to her senses before she'd actually walked down the aisle with the loser, although James still struggled to understand what she had ever seen in him in the first place.

"Talking about Mom, did she agree to watch the little angel on date night or do I have that pleasure?"

"Uh, it's okay – Mom's got this one, but if it goes well and there's a second date, you're in the running, buddy."

James threw his head back and laughed. "In the running? I didn't realise it was a competition."

"Are you kidding me? Do you know how many babysitting offers I get for that little heathen?" Maria shook her head. "Honestly, I don't know what the hell people see when they look at her, but it sure as shit isn't the whiny, conniving monster I have to put up with when it's time for her to go to bed."

"Will you behave?" James asked playfully. "You have a five-year-old little darling girl, not the spawn of Satan."

Maria snorted. "Trust me. They are one and the same."

James worked in silence while he made his sister a cup of coffee. When he was done, he placed the cup in front of her and leant back against the counter, watching her take a sip. She groaned as though it was the best thing she'd ever tasted. It had to be better than that instant shit she always offered him when he paid her a visit. James busied himself cleaning glasses and when he finally looked up and met his sister's gaze, she had her head cocked to one side and her lips pursed.

"Are you ready to tell me what's going on?" Maria asked.

"Huh?"

"You frowned your way through the entire making of this coffee and you've been on another planet since. If you're not careful, your face will get stuck that way and then who's gonna want to bone ya?"

"Maria!" *Jesus*. Sometimes James had to wonder if they were really related. James had never met someone so uncouth.

She shrugged. "Besides, you're giving me a headache."

James stared at his sister and tried to understand her

reasoning. He couldn't come up with a logical answer so he had to ask, "My frowning is giving you a headache?"

Maria nodded and took another sip of her coffee. "Yep, it's depressing to look at and depressing things give me a headache. I don't know how much more of it I can take. I've got a date Friday, remember? You're supposed to be encouraging me, not making me want to end it all before I even meet the dude. Come on, out with it. What's got your knickers in a twist?"

James scrubbed his eye with the heel of his hand. "Wonderfully eloquent as always."

"Bullshit. I'm not going to ask you again. If you don't tell me what's up, I'll call in the big guns."

"The big guns?" James asked.

Maria's grin turned positively feral. "Mom."

James let out a weary sigh and met his sister's gaze. "Matt is in town."

Maria had the coffee cup raised to her lips, but after James had spoken she lowered it, reached for his hand and held it in her own. Every trace of humour had disappeared. "Are you okay?"

James shrugged as though he was just fine, but the shaky, "No," that came out of his mouth didn't sound fine at all.

"How do you know he's back? Did he come in here?"

James shook his head. "No, Mom told me she saw him at the hospital. His father passed away. So I went to see him this morning."

Maria gasped. "You went to his house?"

"Yeah, only he wasn't home. I was on my way back here when I passed the turning for the river. I haven't been back there in years and, knowing Matt was back, I felt…well, nostalgic, I guess. I never expected him to be there, but he was. He was right there in our spot."

Maria started to rub soothing circles on the back of James' hand. "What did he say?"

"What could he say? He was pissed, naturally. I can't expect him to ever forgive me for what I did."

His sister frowned. "Why the hell not? What happened between you was a long time ago and it wasn't like you meant what you said or what you did. What did he say when you explained your reasons and told him how you felt?"

James' gaze fell to the floor.

"You stupid asshole!"

"Hey!"

"What? You want me to congratulate you for being a dick? Why didn't you tell him what you told me? You should have told him how scared you were that day and that you felt embarrassed. You know that might have been what he wanted to hear."

"And it might not. You were right—what happened between us was a long time ago. Matt has no doubt moved on with his life since then. He probably doesn't give a shit how sorry I am or why I said those things to him ten years ago. He's a twenty-eight-year-old adult now, not a teenager. He has a life, a life that has nothing to do with me or who he was back then. What difference would it make what I said to him now? It wouldn't change anything. Besides, he's only in town to sort out the arrangements for his pop's funeral and then he'll be going back to his life in Des Moines."

"Did he tell you that?"

James frowned. "He didn't have to."

"Right, and I bet you didn't even tell him you went to Des Moines to see him, did you?"

James couldn't look his sister in the eye. He swallowed down a lump in his throat and turned to unload the dishwasher. When he wasn't facing her it became easier to talk, but when the words left his mouth they sounded sad and gloomy.

"What would be the point? He made his feelings clear. I have to respect them." What he sounded was pathetic and he knew it. He half expected his sister to tell him to shut the hell up with the pity party.

"What you have to do is be honest with Matt for once in your life. You drove for over six goddamn hours to see him and to make it right between you — not once but twice, James. *Twice!*"

"Christ, will you drop it already? I don't want to talk about this anymore. Enough, please!" James was starting to lose his temper with his sister even though it was really himself he was angry with. He knew how much of a coward he'd been. He didn't need Maria to remind him of that fact. He was more than capable of chastising himself.

Yes, he'd driven up to Iowa to see Matt a couple of times. But each time he'd got there, he had chickened out of talking to Matt and hadn't even let him know he was there. The last time he'd made the journey was going to be *the* time. He'd had it all figured out in his head. He'd known exactly how he was going to apologise for what he'd said and done. He'd known what he was going to say if Matt questioned him. His strategy had been crystal clear. But then he'd seen Matt embrace a man he'd let into his apartment, and James had had to rethink everything.

Matt had looked happy, and James had had to ask himself what the hell he was doing there. It had been obvious Matt had moved on with his life and forgotten about the past, just as James should have done. Only he hadn't, had he? He couldn't. How the hell was he supposed to move on with his life when every single man he met he compared to the first boy he had ever loved? His Matty.

Chapter Three

Matt leant back in the chair and closed his eyes. He had so much work to do, but after his run-in with James, he didn't have the energy for any of it. He felt drained. He couldn't believe how much the meeting had affected him. He'd tried hard over the years to put James out of his mind, but he clearly hadn't been as successful as he'd thought. Just one look at James was all it had taken to make Matt feel like the pathetic boy he'd been, desperately in love with someone who would never love him back. How had he never seen what an idiot he was? To make matters worse, James had looked great. He'd hardly changed at all over the past ten years except to get even better looking. Damn him.

His wavy blond hair was slightly longer than he used to wear it and it was slightly darker, probably because James didn't spend as much time in the sun as he had when they'd been in high school. His build was the same. James had never been bulky, but solid. Tall and lean—an almost athletic build to him even though he'd never been interested much in sports. His face had been the same, filled out a little more and having lost its boyishness, but he was still handsome. Even more so…

The sound of knocking tore Matt from his thoughts and reluctantly he got up to answer the front door. He prayed that it wouldn't be James again, because he wasn't in the right frame of mind to deal with him. He didn't have the energy to fight anymore, but the scariest part was that he wasn't even sure he wanted to fight with James. He'd made his feelings perfectly clear, though. So there was no way James would be coming around any time soon. He wouldn't have the balls.

But that meant whoever was at the door was more than likely calling by to see his pop and hadn't heard about what had happened. And how would they? Matt hadn't even thought about informing his pop's friends about his death. Damn. That was another thing to put on his to-do list. He knew of a few people his pop had kept in touch with over the years, but he'd need his address book to find the rest. He'd look for it later.

He strode down the hall and pulled open the door. Before he could speak, he was met with a high-pitched squeal and enveloped in a bone-crushing hug that nearly knocked him from his feet.

"Laney? That you?" Matt hadn't had a chance to see the woman's face before he was buried beneath a mass of thick auburn curls.

The woman pulled back and studied his face. "Of course it's me, dumbass, who did you think it was?"

Matt grinned. "It's good to see you, too."

"Why didn't you tell me you were coming home? I'd have made sure I was here. I mean, I know I am here, but… Aww hell, you know what I mean. Did you and your pop make up?"

Laney was the only person from Providence that Matt kept in touch with. Although they'd grown up just across the street from each other, they hadn't been close in high school. It wasn't that they disliked each other or didn't have anything in common, just that Matt had spent all his time with James and he hadn't had the time or inclination to make any other friends. But Matt and Laney had ended up going to the same college together, and because they'd both been new and had felt like fish out of water, they'd struck up a friendship that had lasted ever since, even though they were now living in different states.

Laney was the first person Matt had told he was gay. Well, that was if he didn't include the botched kiss with James as telling someone about his sexuality. He'd been nervous about telling her, especially after what had happened with James, but that had made him even more determined to get it all off his chest. He'd brought it up in casual conversation one day shortly after they'd started hanging out in college. Matt had wanted to get it over with before they became friends, because he hadn't wanted to get close to her and get hurt again if she didn't like what she discovered later. Laney had shrugged, said, "That's cool," then taken another sip of her soda. That had been the end of the conversation.

But as Matt looked at Laney's happy face and her last comment sank in, it was clear she hadn't heard about his father's death, and Matt hadn't thought to call her and tell her. He didn't know how to say the words now, either. They were stuck in his damn throat.

"How did you know I was back?" he asked instead.

"I didn't. I was home visiting my mom and I saw your car parked in the drive. Is everything okay? You look tired."

Matt shook his head then took a deep breath and tried to get his mouth to form the words. "It's Pop, Laney. He died. He…"

Before Matt could get out another word, Laney had him crushed in another tight embrace that damn near stole all the breath from his lungs.

"Oh God, Matt honey, I'm so sorry," she mumbled against his neck.

Laney's grip on him was so tight Matt couldn't do much more than shrug and try to swallow the painful lump in his throat.

"Come in," he managed at last. "I'll make coffee."

Ten minutes later they were seated at the kitchen table, already drinking their second cup. Matt filled Laney in on everything that had happened since he'd got the phone call at work.

"You've been through so much in the last couple of days. You shouldn't have had to go through any of it alone. Why the hell didn't you call me? You idiot."

Matt shrugged. "I didn't know you were home," he said

lamely. Truth was, he didn't know why he hadn't called his friend. He'd done a lot of things that were out of character in the past twenty-four hours. Maybe it was the grief.

Laney gave him the look. "You think I wouldn't have come home? Jesus, Matt, you're my best friend. And I'm only living in Kansas, for Chrissake. It's hardly on the other side of the world. I'd have come home in a heartbeat. I'll always be here for you."

Matt reached out and covered Laney's hand with his own. "You're here now."

Laney nodded and took a sip of her coffee. "So, he finally apologised, did he?"

Matt nodded. "Yeah. Not that it makes any difference. I don't want his damn apology."

Laney raised her eyebrows but stayed silent. She held Matt's gaze for a few moments until he was squirming in his seat.

"Okay, okay, it does make a difference. You happy now?" Sometimes Matt hated how well Laney had come to know him over the years. It meant he couldn't hide anything from her, not that he ever had anything that needed hiding.

"Marginally," Laney replied. "You can try to fool yourself, but you don't fool me. I can see right through your pretence and don't you forget it. And thank God that despicable, sorry excuse for a human being is out of your life. I was hoping *you'd* kick *him* to the kerb, but this works just fine too. At least he's gone. Maybe now you can meet someone that gives a shit about you and preferably someone with a backbone, who's not afraid to tell the world you're together. You deserve better than that, Matt."

Matt nearly choked on his coffee. "I thought you liked Tom!"

Laney snorted. "Tolerated is more like it, for your sake. Liked? Please. Give me some credit. I do have a little taste, you know."

Matt put his cup down on the table and sighed. "I've made a real mess of things, haven't I?"

"No, sweetie, you haven't. You just never got over the boy you were in love with when you were a teen. It's not a bad thing to be so steadfast and committed, but it usually helps if that person loves you back, you know?"

Matt's first instinct was to protest, to deny that he still had feelings for his best friend after all these years, but he knew it would be futile to lie to Laney. She was too damn sharp for her own good.

Matt's shoulders slumped in defeat. "What am I going to do now?"

"Well, for starters, we've got a funeral to arrange."

"We?" Matt's voice shook, but he didn't look away from Laney's penetrating gaze. He couldn't.

Laney frowned. "You didn't think I was going to let you do this all on your own, did you? I'm staying, for as long as you need me."

"What about your job?"

Laney gave a slight shrug of her shoulders. "They can manage without me for a while longer. I'm due time off anyway. I work too damn hard and they wouldn't dare argue with me. They know what side their bread is buttered on."

Matt quickly got out of his chair and threw his arms around Laney. "You're one in a million, you know that?"

Laney chuckled. "I know, I know, but can you tell my husband that, please? Just in case he didn't get the memo?"

Matt laughed then, couldn't help himself. "That man couldn't love or spoil you any more if he tried."

When Laney pulled back to meet Matt's gaze, her grin was positively wicked. "Matt, honey. There's *always* room for improvement on the spoiling front and don't you forget it. We wouldn't want Steve to get complacent now, would we?"

Matt shook his head, a small smile playing on his lips. "No, we definitely wouldn't want that."

"Okay, enough of this chit-chat, we have a busy day ahead of us. What's the first thing you have to get done?"

"I have to call Pop's lawyer. Tell him what happened."

Laney nodded. "Okay, you go and call him, and I'll start to give this place a bit of a spruce, how does that sound? When I'm done cleaning, you can put me to work on something else."

Matt smiled gratefully. "Thanks. I mean it, Laney. I can't tell you how much I appreciate your help."

Laney shrugged. "What are friends for if not to give support when you need it? Well okay, and to be a pain in the butt from time to time, but we won't talk about that now."

Larry was surprised to hear from Matt, but the lawyer quickly got down to business when he learnt of his old friend's death. Larry and Hank had been the same age and they were both Providence natives. They'd been on the football team together in high school and had gone to the same college. Matt had seen a lot of Larry when he was growing up because his father and Larry had kept in touch over the years. They had been drinking buddies, and Larry and his wife had been a part of the furniture on game nights.

Matt made an appointment to call by his office at four that afternoon. He made a little small talk, but for the most part Matt didn't have a lot to say to the older man. He didn't dislike him, but other than Matt's father, they didn't have a whole hell of a lot in common.

When he finished talking to Larry, Matt helped Laney clean the house. Matt usually hated cleaning, but it was nice to have something to do that didn't require the use of too many brain cells. He was happy not to have to think too much, because his thoughts inevitably turned to his father's death or to James — two things he couldn't allow himself to think about if he wanted to hold it together.

Matt's father had been a dentist and, even though he'd retired several years ago, he was still well-known around town. Matt imagined when people heard of his father's death they would start showing up to pay their respects, so Matt wanted the house to be spotless because that was the sort of thing people noticed when they paid someone a visit, wasn't it?

By the time they'd finished the cleanup, Matt's stomach was growling loudly, reminding him how hungry he was.

Laney chuckled when she heard it. "You not had anything to eat today?"

Matt shook his head. "No, I couldn't face it this morning. Stomach didn't feel right."

Laney shot Matt another one of those looks that made him feel about five years old. How did she manage that? He felt the urge to apologise even though he didn't know what he should apologise for.

"I'm not surprised your stomach didn't feel right," she said. "I could smell the booze on you as soon as you opened the door, but I didn't want to say anything."

Matt's eyebrows lifted in surprise. "*You* didn't want to say anything? Why the hell not? I've never known you not to speak your mind before."

She shrugged. "I thought you deserved to be cut some slack, but if I smell it on you tomorrow, you can rest assured, buddy, that you and I are going to have some serious words. I'll not have you drowning your sorrows while I'm around. Got it?"

Matt's mouth curved up against his will. "You don't have to worry. If I never have a glass of whisky again it will be too damn soon."

Laney nodded. "That's good enough for now, I suppose. Shall we go out to grab some lunch?"

"Oh, I don't know, Lane," Matt hedged. "I'm not really up to seeing people and I have to meet with Pop's lawyer later."

Laney strode across the room and stood in front of Matt. She lifted his chin until he met her eye. "You might not want to go out or to see people at all, but trust me, Matt— it's the best thing you could do. You can't shut yourself away in this house. The sooner you start getting out there, the better. And it's only lunch, hon. We don't have to go anywhere fancy. There's a diner in town, we could grab something quick there. I haven't been in before, but my mom said the food is pretty good. And you're not meeting Larry until four, we have plenty of time."

Matt gave Laney a tired smile. He had to love her for trying and deep down he knew she was right. He couldn't just sit in the house staring at four walls and surrounded by his father's things. That would be a sure-fire way of making him feel depressed.

"Okay, let's go to lunch."

"Attaboy. Give me ten minutes to run home and change my clothes, and I'll meet you out front, okay?"

"In Laney speak, that's 'give me half an hour'," Matt joked.

Laney made a great show of looking offended, but she didn't say anything further before she ducked out of the door. There was nothing she could say – Matt had been spot on.

* * * *

Matt parked in the lot outside the diner and met Laney around the front of the car. He'd never been to the diner before, either – had never seen it even – so it couldn't have been open for more than a couple of years, because he would have remembered it. Even though he'd lived away from Providence for ten years, not a lot had changed. But this place...this place looked new. And there was something about its name. It struck a chord with Matt – made him remember something that hadn't crossed his mind in a while.

"The Lucky Dollar?" Laney asked sceptically as though she'd been reading Matt's thoughts. "Sounds like the name of a casino, not a diner."

Matt nodded. "Do you know who owns it?"

"Nope, not a clue, why?"

"Oh, it's nothing," Matt said. "It looks nice."

Laney nodded her agreement and pushed open the glass-paned door. Matt followed her inside. She'd barely taken two steps into the bright and welcoming room before she turned and starting pushing Matt back towards the door.

"Uh, come on, we can eat somewhere else."

"Huh? Why? What's the—?" Matt's words cut off when he looked across to the counter and saw James staring back at him. "Crap."

"Come on, Matt, let's go."

Matt held James' gaze and it became almost like a game to see who would look away first. The reason for the name of the diner became suddenly clear, but knowing why it had been given that name made a blush spread across Matt's face. Why would James call his business after something that was so personal to the two of them?

Matt had given James the dollar when they were twelve years old. It had been a gift from his father—a 1976 Eisenhower dollar. There was nothing unusual about it as far as Matt had been aware. There were still many of them in circulation, but Matt's father had told him he'd won the dollar and that it was 'lucky'. Matt had scoffed at that idea and his father never did tell him how he had come to win it, but when James' baby sister Maria had come down with pneumonia, Matt had given his best friend the dollar and his sister had pulled through. Of course, Matt knew now that Maria's improved health had most likely been down to the miracle of medicine rather than the healing powers of an old coin. But twelve-year-old Matt had believed the hype, as had James. And from then on they had passed the dollar back and forth to each other whenever they'd needed a little luck.

"Matt?" Laney said, pulling Matt from his recollections. "Come on, let's leave."

"Matt, is that you?" Reluctantly he tore his gaze from James' face and turned to see who had called out his name. Maria, James' little sister, was striding in their direction. Her thick, long brown hair was flapping wildly behind her.

"Matt! That is you! Come here and give me a big old hug, will ya?"

Matt smiled and took the much smaller woman in his arms. "Hey, Maria, it's been a while. How have you been keeping?" Matt asked when they finally separated.

"I've been doing great. I've got a monster of a daughter now, she's five already."

Matt smiled indulgently and said, "They grow up quick, don't they?" Not that he had the first clue about how quickly children grew up, but he'd heard it said a time or two and it sounded about right.

Maria rolled her eyes. "Don't even get me started." Maria became serious suddenly. "I'm sorry to hear about your dad."

"Thanks." Matt wasn't sure what else to say. There wasn't a lot you could say under the circumstances, so he indicated his best friend and asked Maria, "Do you remember Laney, from high school?"

Maria finally looked over Matt's shoulder and noticed Laney stood behind him. "Well, hello stranger," she cooed, practically shoving Matt out of the way to get a hug.

Matt watched the two women chatter on about babies and husbands or lack thereof with a bemused expression. He kept up with most of their chatter, but they lost him somewhere between breastfeeding and cutting in a first tooth. Matt shuddered and tuned out of the conversation, his gaze drifting to James' wide shoulders and muscular-looking chest. He'd tried his utmost not to stare, but it seemed his body was a damned traitor because not only was he staring, he was walking in James' direction on legs that seemed to have a will of their own.

"I…"

"I…" Matt and James said in unison.

James chuckled nervously and rubbed the back of his neck. "You go first."

"I didn't know you worked here," Matt said. "If I'd have known, I wouldn't have come in."

James' smile faded. He looked almost wounded, but he recovered quickly. "I own the place. Bought it a couple of years ago, and whether you want to come in here or not, you'll always be welcome."

Matt shrugged and tried not to notice the sparkle of light in James' eyes or the fullness of his mouth. He looked over his shoulder to see if Laney and Maria had stopped gossiping so he could get the hell out of there, because being in such close proximity to James was awakening feelings Matt had put to bed a long time ago, or so he'd thought. But when he turned, the two women had their heads locked together and were deep in a conversation that looked to be for their ears only. Matt sighed.

"Can I get you a cup of coffee?" James asked.

Matt was tempted to say no just to spite James, but then he realised the only person he would be spiting was himself. James probably wouldn't give two hoots whether he drank his coffee or not.

He nodded his head, but the "Thank you," he supplied was harder to voice.

"Take a seat," James said and started to make the coffee.

Matt scowled. James' words sounded too much like a command. He didn't like James telling him what to do, but he knew he'd look like an idiot if he kept standing like he was in line for a bus, so he reluctantly sat on one of the red leather stools and tried hard not to stare at his old friend while he made the coffee. He didn't manage it. The years really had been kind to James. He'd been so surprised to see James at the lake he hadn't got a good look at him, but now he couldn't stop. Although James was still tall and lean, his shirt looked as though it hid muscles that sixteen-year-old James could only have dreamt of possessing. Yep, James had certainly filled out in all the right places. His gaze drifted lower. *Damn.*

"You want cream in this?" James asked, pointing to the cup.

Matt squirmed on the stool. *Crap.* Had James caught him

staring at his ass? Wouldn't that be so damn typical?

He shook his head. "No thanks, I take it black."

James raised a curious eyebrow but he didn't comment. He'd hated black coffee when he'd been younger and wondered if James had remembered that. James placed the cup on the counter in front of Matt and picked up one of his own. Matt took a sip of the hot liquid and nearly groaned out loud in appreciation. James must have seen the look on his face because he chuckled.

"Good, right?"

Matt shrugged and took another sip. When he thought he could speak without making an idiot of himself, he looked up and met James' gaze. "So... The Lucky Dollar, huh?"

James' gaze never left his, even when he put the coffee down and reached into his jeans pocket. He retrieved the dollar and threw it at Matt. Matt caught it deftly and turned the coin over in his hand.

"You still carry this?"

James' mouth curved up into a small smile. "Every day."

Matt slid the coin back across the counter, but James shook his head. "No, it already brought me my share of luck. I figure it's your turn to carry it for a while."

"What luck did it bring you?" Matt heard himself asking.

When James replied, his voice was low and rough sounding, but it was the words themselves that made Matt shiver. "It brought you home," James said.

Matt ignored the increased thudding of his heart and how his breath caught in his chest, but he couldn't ignore the way his dick hardened against his will. Matt did a mental eye-roll. Stupid, damn treacherous body. Didn't it know now wasn't the time or the place to appreciate the scenery? What had James meant by that exactly anyway? Why would he give a damn that Matt had come home? Matt was still squirming uncomfortably under James' intense gaze when Laney tapped him on the shoulder.

"Everything okay?"

He tore his eyes away and looked over his shoulder to

where Laney was watching him with a great big smile on her face. Anyone who didn't know her would think she was perfectly at ease, but Matt knew her well. The stiff set to her shoulders and the somewhat wary look in her eyes were the only indications of her unease. But Matt had learnt to interpret her expressions well over the years.

"Yeah," he reassured. "I'm good."

Only when she seemed satisfied with his answer did she turn her attention from Matt. "Hello, James," she said in as friendly a voice as James was likely to get. Matt loved that she felt so loyal to him.

"Laney. It's good to see you back in town," James said. "Can I get you a cup of coffee?"

Laney hesitated for a moment before nodding her head. "Sure. Thanks."

Maria made herself comfortable on the stool next to Matt's. She was grinning broadly, her head swivelling back and forth between Matt and her brother, watching their interaction with interest. When James finally turned to make Laney's coffee, she spoke.

"So how has life been treating you, Matt? You have a boyfriend?"

Matt gaped at Maria. He didn't know why he was so surprised by her directness, but she'd caught him off guard. James had stopped what he was doing, his back stiff and ramrod straight as though he, too, was waiting on Matt's reply, almost as though the answer was important to him.

"I've been good," Matt answered. "And no, I'm not seeing anyone at the moment." Months of dating a man who was still in the closet had made the answer practically automatic and it was only after he'd spoken that Matt stopped to think about Tom and their recent breakup—if he could call it that. Was it a breakup if your partner had never considered you to be in a relationship in the first place? Matt watched James relax his shoulders in his peripheral vision.

"Oh, I'm sorry to hear that," Maria said, although she didn't look sorry at all—she looked pleased.

"What about you, Maria?" Laney asked. "How come you're not married?"

Maria sighed. "Me? I'm still waiting on Mr Right. Thought I'd found him, but it didn't work out." She shrugged. "Actually I'm going on a date on Saturday night that has potential. Hey, why don't you both come over for dinner on Friday night? Then you can help me pick out what to wear and meet my little monster at the same time. What do you say, Matt?" Maria looked at him expectantly.

"Uh, I don't know. I've got a lot going on at the moment... You know, with the funeral arrangements and..."

"That's exactly why you should come," Maria said. "It's a difficult time and I know how easy it can be to forget to eat. The last thing you want to do is stay home on your own."

"I..." Matt looked at Laney, hoping she would help him get out of the invitation, but she'd taken a sudden interest in the contents of a menu. James was still busy making the coffee. Matt didn't want to be rude and in the end he figured it wouldn't do any harm to go to her house for a bite to eat, so he nodded his agreement. "Sure, I'd love to come to dinner."

Maria's face lit up. "Perfect. I'll cook you my speciality. Pasta with spicy meatballs in a tomato and red wine sauce. You'll love it. Laney, can you make it to dinner?"

"Sounds great, but I already promised my mom we could have a girlie day on Friday night—dinner and a movie. I don't want to back out because we don't see each other often since I moved to Kansas."

Maria waved off Laney's concerns. "No worries. I'm sure Matt here can help me choose an outfit, can't you, Matt?"

Matt smiled politely, but he had to wonder what the hell he'd let himself in for.

Chapter Four

James rubbed his sweaty palms on jean-clad knees and crossed the room to the front window to peer out onto the street.

"Will you relax already? You're going to wear a hole in my carpet."

James rolled his eyes. "You have wooden floors."

"You know what I meant," Maria said with a swish of her hand.

"Are you sure Matt knows I'm going to be here for dinner tonight?"

"Quit worrying, James, it's going to be fine."

James' stomach did a somersault. "Why aren't you answering my question? What did Matt say when you told him I'd be here?"

"Hope, will you pick your toys up, please? You know Mommy has a friend coming to dinner. Hope!"

James watched his sister run around the room after the over-excitable five-year-old. When Maria finally got Hope seated and quiet, James tried again. "Maria? What did Matt say *exactly*?"

"Huh?"

"Matt. What did he say when you told him I'd be here for dinner?"

Maria ducked behind Hope, suddenly becoming very interested in a cache of dolls near the sofa that were missing various limbs.

"Oh God." Just as the words left his mouth, Matt's car turned into his sister's driveway. "Oh God. You didn't tell him, did you?"

Maria met his gaze and had the good grace to look embarrassed. "Uh, it might have slipped my mind."

"Maria! How could you? Oh God."

"Will you just relax already? Jeez."

"He's going to hate me," James said morosely.

"He already hates you," Maria said. "Tonight is going to make him like you again."

The doorbell sounded just before James went into full-blown panic mode, and Maria jumped up and strode through the living room and out into the hall. James leaned against the wall and tried to blend in with the floral wallpaper. He slid down a little, trying to make himself as small as possible, as though he could hide the fact he was in the room. Matt was going to be pissed off. It was unlikely he'd leave, because Matt wasn't the sort of person who would do something that rude to Maria, and James knew his sister was counting on that. One thing was for sure—Matt wouldn't be thanking Maria any time soon. Throttling her, maybe. He could get in line.

"And this is the little monkey," James heard Maria introduce in the hall. James was so preoccupied he hadn't even noticed Hope follow her mom out to the door.

"Well hello, gorgeous," Matt said brightly. Just the sound of his voice made butterflies dance in James' stomach and sent shivers of delight gliding down his spine. He'd missed that voice. God had he missed it. He wouldn't be too proud to admit it either. Well, maybe not too proud, but too embarrassed certainly.

James' eyes were riveted to the door. He couldn't have looked away if his life depended on it. His body was tight with anticipation. A moment later Maria walked into the room followed by Hope, who was tugging Matt along beside her.

"Look who's here, Uncle James," Hope said. "This is Mommy's friend, Matt."

"Oh, so it is," James said to his niece.

James lifted his gaze to Matt's face and his breath caught

73

in his throat. Matt's first reaction was one of surprise, but it disappeared quickly and his brow furrowed.

"I didn't realise you were going to be here." Matt's voice was steady and showed no trace of emotion, but James could see how taut his body had become—his shoulders tense and his back stiff and straight.

"Yeah, guess it must have slipped Maria's mind, eh, sis?" James shot a glare at his sister.

Maria shrugged. "You know me, terrible memory. Take a seat, Matt."

"Thanks." It was obvious how uncomfortable Matt was with the entire situation and James felt for him—he really did—but he couldn't help but be happy to have another chance to express his regret to Matt. Because *he did* regret what he had done to Matt all those years ago. He'd never regretted anything more. His biggest desire, one he didn't dare hope for, was that he and Matt could become friends again.

Maria waited until Matt was seated then she grabbed hold of Hope and lifted her until she was draped on one hip. "I've got to put the monster to bed. It's past her bedtime already, but I promised her she could stay up until you got here. Fix Matt a drink, James. I won't be long."

"No!" Hope protested, frantically trying to slide out of her mother's tight hold. "I don't want to go to bed!"

"Pointless arguing, you're going." Maria's tone brooked no argument, but Hope was almost as stubborn as her mother. She squirmed in Maria's arms, trying to get her mother to release her.

"Please," she whined. "You promised, Mommy. You said I could stay up past bedtime!"

"Yes, and you already did. It was bedtime an hour ago."

The devastation on Hope's face as Maria carried her from the room pulled at James' heartstrings...until Hope started kicking and screaming and crying, then all James felt was relief he didn't have any children of his own. Hope was wonderful in small doses, but how Maria coped with her twenty-four-seven James had no idea. When the sounds of Hope's cries disappeared up the stairs, James became suddenly aware that he and Matt were alone.

"I should g—"

"I'm sorry," James interrupted.

"You seem to be saying that a lot," Matt scoffed. "What exactly are you sorry for this time?"

James sighed and raked a hand through his thick hair. "I really thought my sister had told you I was going to be here. If I'd known she hadn't, I'd…"

"You'd what? You wouldn't have come? You could always leave."

James scowled. "No, I couldn't. Look, it might not have been the smartest thing my sister has ever done, but she meant well. She just wants us to be friends again and she went to a lot of trouble to cook the meal tonight, so no, I can't just leave. I wouldn't do that to her, even though I want to strangle her. It's only dinner for Chrissake. Can't we just eat it and try to be civil to one another?"

Matt shrugged. "Don't suppose I have any choice."

James pushed off the wall and crossed the room until he stood in front of Matt. "You always have a choice, Matt, but I'd like it if you stayed."

"Why?"

James was tempted to give a cop-out answer. He could have said he didn't want to hurt his sister's feelings, but even though that was partly the truth, it wasn't the whole of it and James didn't want to lie to Matt, even if it was a lie by omission. "Because I'd like it if we can be friends again, too," he said, holding Matt's gaze. "Now that we're both here, can we try to get along, please?"

They stared at one another for what felt like an eternity but couldn't have been more than ten seconds. Matt tore his gaze away and James saw him swallow before he answered.

"Fine."

James nodded, relieved. "What can I get you to drink?"

"Beer's fine."

James nodded and went to retrieve two beers from the kitchen. He took a deep breath before he re-entered the room and handed one of the beers to Matt.

"Here you go."

Matt took the beer and lifted it in a silent 'thank you'. The minutes ticked on while they both drank their beer in silence. James wanted to say something to lift the unease, but he didn't think Matt would appreciate small talk so he stayed silent and continued to drink his beer. Much to James' surprise, it was Matt who finally broke the silence.

"What are we doing here, James?"

When James looked up and saw the raw emotion that could only have been anger in Matt's eyes, it felt like a punch to the gut.

"What do you mean?"

"This... Us..." Matt said, waving a hand between them. "You think a shared beer is going to erase everything that's gone between us? You think that's all it takes?"

James sighed and lowered his eyes. "Whatever you might think, this wasn't my idea, okay? But now that we're here..."

Matt snorted. "Whatever. I think it's really low of you to use your sister and niece for this sorry excuse for... whatever the hell this is."

"Hey! Now wait just a damn minute! I would never use either my sister or my niece just to make a damn apology. I'm perfectly capable of doing that on my own, as I think I proved earlier. How dare you say that? You don't even know me!"

"And whose fault is that?" Matt snapped.

"Hey, will you two keep the noise down? They can hear you two streets over and I've just put Hope to bed. If you don't want an irritable five-year-old and a grouchy mommy then I suggest you cut this shit out right now!"

James stared at his sister open-mouthed. Man, did she have a temper on her.

"Sorry," Matt mumbled.

"Uh, yeah, sorry, sis."

Maria shot daggers at them both. "Now do you think it's safe for me to go and check on the pasta or will I get back to find you've torn each other apart?"

James chanced a look at Matt before he answered, "It's safe."

As soon as Maria left the room again, James turned to Matt. They hadn't got off on the best foot and he thought it would be better to get the subject off them and onto safer ground. "How was the meeting with your pop's lawyer?" he asked.

Matt's shoulders slumped. He took another drink of his beer before he spoke. "He left me everything. The house, money, investments — everything he had came to me."

James frowned. "You sound as though you didn't expect it. Who else did you think he'd leave it all to?"

"Pop and I hadn't spoken in a couple of years," Matt said quietly. "I guess I thought he might have changed his will. I don't know. Maybe I'm just being dumb."

"You hadn't spoken?" That was news to James and he'd seen Matt's dad several times over the years. He'd never mentioned they'd fallen out.

Matt shook his head. "No. I mean, we'd argued, but I didn't expect it to last. I always thought we'd make up, you know?"

James had to swallow down a blasted lump that had risen in his throat. "Yeah. I know exactly what you mean."

Matt looked up then and met James' gaze. They looked at each other for a long moment and the electricity that thrummed between them was intense. James had to speak, not just to fill the silence but because he was afraid of blurting out something he might later regret. "How come you weren't talking to your father? What did you argue about?"

"I told him I was gay. I guess I thought he already knew, like he was a damn psychic or something, but it couldn't have come as more of a surprise to him. He was pissed.

Said some things…" Matt shrugged. "So did I—bad things. I can't believe I'll never get a chance to tell him I'm sorry, that I didn't mean them. I was just angry, you know? I lashed out."

James could relate to that. It sounded exactly like the situation between him and Matt. He wondered if Matt made the comparison also.

"Your father knew you loved him. He worshipped the ground you walked on. Always did, even though he could be a stubborn old goat sometimes."

Matt shook his head. "You didn't see him this time. I've never seen him so angry. He hated me for what I am."

"I think you're wrong, Matt. When I went to see him he had nothing but praise for you. He told me all about your job and his smile when he spoke about you…" James shook his head. "He was so very proud of you."

The shock on Matt's face was clear. "When was that?"

"I spoke to him a lot over the years. The last time was just two or maybe three weeks ago."

"But we hadn't spoken in over two years."

James shrugged. "He never told me that. Just said how proud of you he was."

"You said you went to see him. What did you go to see him for?"

Trust Matt to ask the only question James didn't want to answer. But there was no point in lying or trying to hide what he'd done. James *couldn't* lie to Matt, even to save his own pride. "I went to ask him for your address in Iowa."

Matt's eyebrows knitted together. "What did you want with my address?"

"I wanted your address so that I could go and see you, to apologise and to beg your forgiveness."

Matt snorted. "Really? So why didn't you come?"

James held Matt's gaze with ease. "I did. Twice, matter of fact. But when I turned up you were with your boyfriend, so I left."

Matt's mouth fell open, his face the picture of surprise.

78

"Hey guys, dinner's ready!" Maria called.

"Saved by the bell, eh?" James smiled warmly at his old friend. "Come on, better get out there before Maria has a hissy fit about her food getting cold. Trust me, I've seen it and it's not pretty."

James led the way to the kitchen and Matt followed. Before they reached the door, Matt put a hand on James' shoulder, halting his steps.

"Thank you," he whispered.

Matt's hand fell to his side as James turned, but their eyes remained locked.

"Your father loved you. Don't ever doubt that."

* * * *

As Matt shovelled the last forkful of spaghetti into his mouth, Maria poured more wine into his nearly empty glass. He didn't usually drink when he was with company for dinner, because he couldn't handle his alcohol and didn't want to make a fool of himself. But James' revelation had thrown him for a loop and the wine helped calm him. He was already way over the legal limit for driving, so he knew he'd have to take a cab home and come back for his car in the morning. Another glass wouldn't make any difference, would it?

He hadn't spoken to James about what he'd told him earlier because he didn't want to discuss it in front of Maria. He couldn't believe his father hadn't mentioned their argument and had spoken about him as though he were proud of him. Could it be true? Was that what the old man had really thought of him? Then why had he been so damn stubborn? But Matt was hardly one to talk about being stubborn, especially with James sitting across the table from him, trying his best to make amends.

Matt couldn't even bring himself to think about James' admission. How could he have driven all the way to Des Moines not once but *twice* without actually telling Matt he was there? And why would he go to all that trouble? He couldn't understand that. James must have seen him with Tom on one of the rare occasions Tom had come to his house. What were the odds on that?

Tom had hardly ever gone to Matt's house because he'd been afraid that someone he knew would see him leaving early in the morning. Tom had cared too damn much what people thought about him. Matt had once believed he could help Tom come to terms with who he was, but he realised now the man was never going to change and would probably never accept it. If he was considering getting married to a woman, then he wasn't even close to that stage.

"How was the spaghetti?" Maria asked, after she'd finished pouring the wine.

"It was really good." Matt wiped his mouth with a napkin then smiled at his host. "I had no idea you could cook so well."

"Neither did I," James said, only to get a slap on the shoulder from his sister.

"I never used to cook at all," she said. "But when I had Hope I figured I should learn. I didn't want her growing up to live on takeout like I pretty much did all the way through college. I took some lessons and what do you know? Turns out I didn't suck as much as I thought I did."

"Maria's in the middle of her dissertation at the moment," James said proudly.

"No kidding? You're doing a doctorate?"

"Yep, and it's kicking my ass."

Matt chuckled. "How do you find the time to study, take care of Hope and look after this place?"

James leaned in close and Matt tried to ignore the heat that radiated from James or how his breath fanned against Matt's neck. "You forgot her part-time job at the library," he said, and Matt very nearly moaned when James' low, husky voice sent shivers down his spine. "Didn't you know my sister is a machine?"

Maria let out a very unladylike snort, essentially putting an end to Matt's thoughts about some other ways James could make him moan. Jesus, he'd been having thoughts about James all through dinner and the wine wasn't helping any. It was making him relax too much, making him let down his guard and James was being too damn nice. If he still hated him like he had that day back just after high school, Matt could deal with that, but this new and improved James he had no clue how to handle. Or was this just the old James? The one he'd grown up with. The one he'd been friends with from second grade on. Maybe James hadn't changed at all. Maybe he really had been acting out of character that day by the river, and he hadn't meant what he'd said and what he'd done. Maybe Matt had scared him that day and he'd struck out. But why hadn't he apologised before now? It still rankled that James hadn't had the courage to tell him he was sorry much sooner, especially as he'd driven all the way up to Des Moines to tell him.

"Must run in the family, because you work just as hard and there's no stopping Mom either," Maria said. "What about *your* job, Matt? Are you going straight back to work after the funeral?"

Matt took a sip of his wine before he spoke. "Actually, I quit my job right before I came home so I've got nothing to go back to, except my house. I haven't decided yet if I'm going to go back at all."

"Really?" The tone of James' voice was hopeful and his face was full of surprise. "You're thinking of staying here, for good?"

When their gazes locked, James' face was covered with the hope Matt had heard in his voice.

Matt shrugged. "It's an option and I've got to think about Pop's house now, too. It's pointless keeping both houses on. Pop owned his outright, so if I'm not going to live in it then I need to think about putting it on the market and I don't think I'm ready to make a decision like that right now."

"Well, I think you should stay," Maria said. "This is your

home and you have friends here, people that care about you. You could be happy living here again. And of course you're always welcome here anytime you want a home-cooked meal."

"You know, I'm not such a bad cook myself," Matt said.

James' smile was bright. It caused a shiver to run the length of Matt's body. "Really? Maybe I'll call on your services when I need help in the diner."

Matt grinned. "Oh, I'm not *that* good. I can just about hold my own."

"You know, you should listen to Maria about staying here in Providence. She's usually right."

Maria chuckled. "And don't you forget it."

When Matt looked down, he realised his wineglass was empty again. *Jesus.* Just how much had he had to drink tonight? He'd lost count of the amount of times Maria had topped up his glass and he was sure he'd seen her open a second bottle. She was hardly drinking herself and James wasn't drinking at all.

"You don't drink?" he asked, nodding at James' ice water.

"I do, but I need to be at the diner early in the morning for a delivery so I figured it would be better if I didn't drink at all. I know what I'm like. One would have turned into two and before you know it I'd be saying bye-bye to the delivery."

"Actually, I'm going to have to think about calling a cab." Matt looked at his watch and groaned. "It's starting to get late."

"Nonsense," James said firmly. "I'll drive you home."

"That's okay. I wouldn't want to be any trouble, I'll just call a cab and…"

"Let him drive you," Maria said with a swish of her hand. "My brother lives to play the Good Samaritan, don't you, James?"

James scowled at his sister. "There's nothing wrong with wanting to help out a friend."

Matt was tempted to point out that they weren't friends

anymore, but after dinner, he just didn't know if that was the truth. James did seem genuinely sorry about what had happened between them in the past and although Matt could be pretty stubborn he didn't want to hold a grudge forever. What would that achieve other than making him miserable? Hadn't he just been through that with his father? Maybe it was time to forgive and forget. Or was that the damn alcohol talking?

Was Matt setting himself up for another fall? He could try to fool himself into believing he and James could just be friends, but he already knew he'd want more from the relationship than James would want to give and where would that leave him? Could he take the chance? Was having a friendship with James again that important to him? Matt didn't have answers to all his questions. He thought maybe the best thing to do for his sanity would be to keep his distance, but when he looked across and took in James' expectant gaze, he realised he'd already made up his mind. He nodded his agreement to his friend's offer of a ride home.

"Thanks, I appreciate it. I'll come by in the morning to pick up my car."

James' smile lit up his face and Matt found himself mirroring it.

"Okay, great."

"I'm going to check on Hope," Maria said, refilling Matt's glass. "Help yourself to more pasta, Matt."

"Thanks, but I couldn't eat another bite, I'm stuffed."

Maria shrugged. "That's okay. It won't go to waste with the human garbage disposal here."

Matt grinned at James' expression of outrage. "Human garbage disposal, eh?" Matt repeated when Maria left the room. "You know, now that I come to think about it, you always did like your food. Weren't you a little overweight in high school?"

"Shut up," James retorted, but the slight curve to his mouth negated his words. "I was never overweight. Besides,

I used to kick your ass in football every damn week."

Matt snorted. "That's hardly cause for celebration. Your mother could probably kick my ass in football."

"Now that's a game I'd pay money to watch."

Matt threw his head back and laughed and it felt good to do so. For a brief moment he was able to forget his troubles and enjoy spending time with James. It reminded him of when they were kids. James had been there at every important moment in Matt's life — be it happy or sad — especially during the sad moments. When his mom had passed away, James had been by his side and had helped him through, lifting his spirits and making him feel better. He was incredibly grateful for that and he wasn't surprised that now, when his pop had died, it was James who was offering comfort and making him smile once again.

James joined in the laughter, the corners of his eyes crinkling. When he met Matt's gaze, his smile was so mesmerising Matt didn't ever want to look away. There was suddenly no air in the room, or had he forgotten to breathe? All he knew was that James was holding his gaze as if by magic — a strong yet invisible force that held them together, a bond that couldn't be broken. Matt felt powerless when looking into James' eyes, like he didn't have control of his own will anymore. It was James' to control, but he felt oddly at ease with that.

James leaned in close until his breath fanned across Matt's face.

"Matt," he whispered hoarsely and Matt found himself holding his breath in anticipation.

"I..."

"She's sleeping like a log," Maria said, striding back into the room. "How we doing on the wine? Shall I open another bottle?"

The spell between them broken at last, Matt reluctantly tore his gaze away from James' face and smiled at Maria. "Are you trying to turn me into a lush?"

Maria giggled. "Too much?"

"A little." Matt nodded. "I should really get going, but we'll have to do this again another night. Maybe next time you can come to mine?"

"Sounds great," Maria said cheerfully and Matt returned her smile.

"James?" Matt asked. "What do you say?"

A trace of surprise flickered across James' face, but he hid it quickly, his mouth instead curving up into a wide, genuine smile. It caused his eyes to sparkle brightly and made him look like the teenager he had been when Matt had last seen him.

"I'd like that." James' voice was thick with emotion and it made Matt forget about every bad thing that had passed between them. "Come on, I'll take you home."

Matt placed a kiss on Maria's cheek then followed James to his car.

As soon as the balmy evening air hit him, Matt's head started to spin and his stomach churned. He knew he'd had a lot to drink, but he didn't think he'd had too much until he'd got up and started moving around. Suddenly everything around him was spinning furiously and Matt had to put a hand on the wall to steady himself.

"You okay?" James came back down the path to stand in front of him. His voice was thick with concern. He placed a steadying hand on Matt's arm and waited until Matt met his gaze. Reluctantly, Matt lifted his head. James looked incredibly handsome in the soft silver beam of the moonlight.

Matt grinned. "You really are a good-looking man, you know that?"

Somewhere in his gut he thought he might regret that later, but the alcohol was making him loose-lipped. A deep frown creased James' brow and he turned his head away. The action went some way to sobering Matt. He took a step back and shrugged off James' hand. His friend's cold reaction wasn't what he'd expected. He should have known better.

"You know, I think I'll walk home. The fresh air will probably do me good," Matt mumbled, stumbling down the driveway past his car. He felt embarrassed. He had to get away.

James grabbed hold of his arm once again, but this time he held on tight when Matt tried to shrug him off.

"Not so fast," James said. "You have any idea how long of a walk it is from here?"

Matt glowered at James. "Of course I know how far it is. I grew up around here, too, remember?"

"How could I forget?"

"What the hell is that supposed to mean?" Matt thought he might be slurring his words, but he was past caring.

"It didn't mean anything," James said. "Come on, get in the car."

Matt tried out a growl and made to move past James' car, but his legs were wobbly so when James led him to the passenger seat, he didn't put up too much of a fight. He didn't even object when James leaned across his body to buckle him in and the intoxicating smell of James' cologne fogged up his senses, making it hard to think clearly. Not that his thoughts were entirely comprehensible after the amount of alcohol he'd consumed.

Watching James walk around the front of the car and slide in next to him, Matt shook his head incredulously. What the hell was he doing? He was acting like the past ten years hadn't happened. Like James hadn't freaked out when Matt had kissed him, hadn't punched him and hadn't called him a fag. He knew James wanted to make amends, but how was Matt supposed to forget something like that? How could he get past it? There had been times throughout dinner when Matt had thought he would be able to forgive James, if not forget, but was he capable of that?

James had been the person Matt had trusted most in the world, but he'd abused that trust and ruined their friendship in the process. Matt knew he couldn't go through that again. Not after everything else he'd been through recently.

He wasn't sure how he'd survive it. Wasn't sure he had the energy to even try.

The next time he tried to focus on their surroundings, James was pulling his car to a stop on the kerb outside Matt's house and not a minute too soon. If the scenery had continued to whizz past his window for much longer, Matt was pretty sure he would have thrown up. James hadn't spoken a single word on the drive back to his house, not that Matt had tried to make conversation either. He would give anything to know what was on James' mind, to understand how he felt. He turned and tried to focus on James' face.

"Thanks for the lift," he slurred, grappling with the seatbelt. What the hell? Was it stuck? He pulled and prodded until James put him out of his misery, leaning across to unclip the belt. Matt ignored the effect the proximity had on his body—well, on his dick to be precise. He nodded his thanks, afraid the tone to his voice would give away his arousal, and made a couple of unsuccessful reaches for the door handle. James looked as though he was trying to hide a smirk, but thankfully he remained quiet. Matt finally got his hand around the handle and pulled. As soon as he made it to the front of the car, James was at his side.

"This is not a date, you know. You don't have to walk me to my damn door," Matt growled and tried to shove James' helping hands away.

James ignored his protests, grabbed hold of his arm and held onto it while they walked the length of the path leading to Matt's front door. James' strong, firm chest pressed up against him as he leaned in near his ear.

"If we were on a date, I'd be doing more than walking you to your door, I can promise you that."

"Cocky bastard!" Matt accused, but his errant cock had other ideas. It liked James' words—a lot more than it should.

James chuckled and kept them upright until they were standing on Matt's porch. "I had no idea it would still be so easy to get a rise out of you."

"Why do you do that? Why antagonise me? What do you

get out of it?"

James shrugged. "I guess it's because I think you're so damn hot when you're angry."

Matt opened his mouth to speak, but the words caught in his throat. He didn't know how he would have responded to that anyway. What the hell was James playing at? He was blowing hot and cold and that was messing with Matt's goddamn head. Did he mean what he'd just said or was it all just a game to him, yet another way to get a rise out of Matt? When James stepped in close, Matt froze, caught by James' magnetic eyes. Even in the moonlight they were captivating. Maybe more so. It sure as hell didn't feel like James was playing a game. There was no way he could fake the hardness in his pants that pressed against Matt's own erection.

James' mouth slowly lifted at the corners. His smile was simply stunning and when James had it trained on Matt it caused his heart to flutter like there was a damned hummingbird trapped in his chest. Tension hung thick in the already heavy, muggy air. James took another step forward until he had Matt pressed up against the door. He placed one hand on Matt's shoulder and the other behind his neck, his fingers sliding into the hair there, making Matt shiver. James must have noticed his reaction because his smile became positively feral. Matt wanted to move away, but he felt paralysed, frozen in place from both fear and desire. He wasn't sure if he'd ever be able to move again.

Heat from James' hand seeped into the back of his neck. It felt as though his skin was sizzling, like James' touch was a personal brand. All the while, their eyes were locked, lost in each other's depths. His whole body threatened to fly apart. It was almost too much for Matt.

"What are you doing?" he breathed, watching in awe as James' lips inched closer to his own.

"Nothing that you don't want," James replied hoarsely. And then he leaned closer and crushed their mouths together. Matt had anticipated the kiss, but it still stole all the breath from his lungs. He couldn't contain the low moan that escaped his throat when James' tongue nudged the seam of his lips, demanding entrance. Matt forgot about everything except how good James' kiss made him feel. James gripped his hair tighter and his cock pressed harder against Matt's. James kissed him as though he'd been born to do just that. His warm, wet tongue felt incredible as it explored the inside of his mouth and coaxed his own tongue into James' mouth. Matt obliged and pretty soon he lost all control and took over the kiss, turning James and pressing him against the door.

"Let's do this inside," Matt breathed against James' mouth.

Pulling in a great lungful of breath, he fished the key out of his pocket and made quick work of opening the door. When he next met James' gaze, the man's eyes were sparkling with mirth.

"What's so funny?"

James sighed. "You have no idea how many times I fantasised about kissing you like that. It used to be every damn day when I was sixteen. Jesus, some days it was all I could think about and, I've got to tell you, the dreams weren't nearly as good as the reality."

Matt felt the heat of a blush creep up his cheeks. "Let's go inside."

James' smile grew wider, but he shook his head. "Not tonight, Romeo." He leant forward and pressed a chaste kiss to Matt's lips then turned and walked back to his car. "See you tomorrow, Matt."

Matt was still standing on his porch, key in hand and mouth agape, when James' car turned the corner at the end of his street. He was equal parts confused as to why he'd be seeing James tomorrow, and annoyed that James was leaving him hanging—or hard as a damn rock, as the case may be.

Chapter Five

James parked his car in Matt's driveway and climbed out. There was a spring in his step that hadn't been there in a long time. He hadn't slept more than a couple of hours the night before, but it hadn't done him any harm. Most of the night he'd tossed and turned—his mind focused solely on that explosive kiss. Jesus, but Matt knew how to kiss. James had been practically weak at the knees and it had been all he could do to pull back and walk away from Matt when he'd invited him inside. His dick had wanted to know what the hell he was doing turning down Matt's offer, but the sensible part of his brain—which had thankfully still been in control—knew that they had to take things slowly.

Matt had just lost his father and James didn't want to take advantage of him when he was vulnerable. So he'd pulled back, walked away and driven home with a dick that was as hard as steel. The rest of the night he'd spent thinking about how good his mouth had felt attached to Matt's and how perfectly their bodies had moulded together as though they were made for one another. And when he'd finally come to his senses, all he could think about was that he'd kissed Matt on his porch, right out in the open where anyone could have seen. Sure it had been dark, but there were a lot of curtain twitchers in Matt's part of town. What if one of them had heard his car pull up and had looked out to see who was there? James didn't want to think about what would happen if people found out he was gay. What would it mean to his business, his livelihood? Would people care? Or would they ostracise him the same way they had Mr Keller, the high school teacher? James couldn't risk that. He needed to be more careful. He couldn't afford to lose his business. He'd invested everything in it.

He jogged up the drive and rapped on the door with his knuckles. A moment later Matt appeared, looking just as sleep-deprived as James had when he'd looked in the mirror that morning. His dark-brown hair was sticking up in tufts and he had lines on his face from the pillow. While James watched, he rubbed his thumb and forefinger over a full day's worth of stubble on his chin. He looked good enough to eat and James suppressed a groan when he felt his dick start to harden.

"Well, don't you look handsome," he commented.

Even though James had been telling the truth, Matt must have taken it as a quip because he practically growled out his reply. "What are you doing here?"

James couldn't contain his grin. Matt wasn't getting rid of him that easily. "Good morning to you, too. I told you I was coming by today. You got any coffee? I didn't have time to grab one at the diner after I took in the delivery. Came straight here." He shouldered past Matt and headed for the kitchen.

"Hey," Matt protested. "Where do you think you're going?"

James turned abruptly, grabbed hold of Matt and planted a big, sloppy kiss on his lips. He let go when they were both breathless and continued on his course to the kitchen. He didn't look back to see if Matt was following him, but he couldn't hear Matt's steps behind him on the hardwood floor. He smiled to himself. *Better get used to it, Matt. I'm here to stay.* He was opening cupboards looking for cups when Matt finally appeared at his side, looking more composed than he had a moment before.

"Look, I don't know what you think you're playing at, but—"

"I'm not."

"Huh?"

"I'm not *playing* at anything. I was an idiot when we were

in high school and I learned my lesson. I missed you, Matt. I missed your friendship. But I'm not prepared to settle for that now. I want more. I want to see where things go between us."

"There is no *us*," Matt said through clenched teeth. "Don't you get that? I think it would be better if you left."

"Better for whom?" James asked. "'Cause it sure as hell wouldn't be better for me, and I don't think it's what you want either."

"You don't have the first damn clue what I want!"

James shrugged. "Maybe, but I know that you've got a funeral to arrange and I'm going to help you do it. Anything else? We'll just have to see how it goes." James sighed and stopped what he was doing. "Look, I know I kissed you — *twice* — but I promise I'm not going to try to rush you into anything, okay? You can take as much time as you want to figure this out. I'm not in any hurry. We need to get to know each other again and that will take time. I know that and I'll wait as long as I have to."

Matt let out a long, weary-sounding breath. "What if I don't want to start anything with you?"

James took a step closer and placed his hand under Matt's chin, lifting it until he met his gaze. "If that's honestly what you want, then I'll respect it — of course I will — but I don't believe it to be true. You couldn't even look me in the eye when you asked that question. I get that you're nervous, Matt — I do. And I realise that you still don't trust me, but give me some time and I'll prove to you that you *can* trust me again. You can count on me."

Matt opened a cupboard to his left and pulled out two cups. "Guess I don't have any choice, do I? Unless you're going to leave?"

"Afraid not."

"Didn't think so."

James hid his grin as he set to work making their coffee, but they barely had time to drink it. Laney was the first person to call by to tell Matt not to bother cooking as she'd be coming over at lunchtime with a pot roast. Then three of Hank's friends showed up one after the other to offer their condolences. Bad news travelled fast in their small town it seemed. Matt was cordial to each of the visitors, but James could tell he just wanted everyone to go away and leave him the hell alone, himself included probably, but James wasn't going to leave him alone at a time like this. No way. He knew how difficult it was coping with a parent's death, but he couldn't begin to imagine having to do that alone.

James knew something about what Matt would be going through, even if he couldn't put himself in Matt's shoes exactly. When his own father had died it had caused an ache in heart he wasn't sure would ever go away. But James had had the rest of his family to lean on. His sisters and mother had been there for each other, offering the type of support that only family and close friends can provide.

Matt had no family left. His grandparents had all died years ago and Matt was an only child like his mother before him. Hank had only one brother that James knew of and he'd died several years ago, having no children of his own. Matt had no one to support him. Well, not any longer because James sure as hell wasn't going anywhere and Maria had told him she was calling by later too. And there was Laney. James didn't know her very well — they hadn't spoken much in high school — but he knew Laney had been friends with Matt all through college and beyond. It was one of the things Hank had told him.

James sat next to Matt at the kitchen table throughout the visit from George Hoskins, the funeral director who had dealt with his own father's funeral. The meeting went as smoothly as could be expected. Matt held it together well throughout the hour-long visit, even though he'd looked pretty lost a couple of times when he'd been asked about flowers and hymns to sing at the service. Several times, James had wanted to reach out and comfort Matt, to take hold of his hand and let him know that he wasn't alone, but he didn't know if Matt would appreciate the gesture in front of George. Mostly he'd been scared that George would tell people about what he'd seen and he hated himself for worrying about that when he should only be concerned about Matt and his problems.

Matt had actually relied on James far more than he'd expected him to. He knew how stubborn Matt could be, but each time the director had asked a question he hadn't been able to answer, he'd turned to James to seek his advice. That in and of itself gave James hope that maybe there was a chance for them after all. And right now he'd take all the hope he could get.

As promised, Laney came by with a pot roast that would put his own mother's to shame. Laney had raised a curious eye at James when he'd answered the door, but she hadn't commented…yet. He supposed she was waiting for the right moment. Laney had been openly friendly towards him, but he could sense her unease with his reappearance into Matt's life. He couldn't blame her. He could tell she was fiercely protective of Matt and he had to respect her for that.

He was loath to admit that Laney and Matt's close relationship made him feel jealous, but he hid it as best he could. He knew he had no right to feel that way. The distance between him and Matt was entirely his own doing and he knew it. They'd just finished eating and Matt had gone to answer the door to yet another caller when Laney cracked, finally speaking her mind.

"What are your intentions towards Matt?"

James nearly choked on a piece of carrot. "My intentions? What are we, in the fifties?"

Laney leant back in her chair and took a sip of water. She didn't reply, but her cool gaze never left James.

James sighed. "I just want to make things right between us. I want us to be friends again."

Laney snorted. "Friends? Don't give me that line of crap. I've seen the way you've been looking at him all through lunch. I'd say you want to be a hell of a lot more than just friends."

James could feel his ears heat and he only hoped his cheeks didn't match. Other than Matt, his sister was the only person he'd told he was gay and that was only because she'd already worked it out and quizzed him about it. Admitting his feelings to Laney felt no easier. He took a deep breath then nodded his head.

"Gaining Matt's trust is important to me. I'd do anything for our friendship to get back to the way it used to be. But I can't lie and say I wouldn't like more. I would."

"So you *are* gay?" Laney came right out and asked. "Even though you broke Matt's nose for kissing you back in high school?"

James had to swallow down the bile that rose in his throat. "I broke his nose?"

"I see that came as a shock."

"Christ, why didn't he say anything?"

Laney's eyebrows lifted almost comically. James might have laughed if his stomach wasn't tied tightly in knots. Right. Why the hell would Matt have told him anything? If their roles had been reversed, James wouldn't have said anything to Matt either. He'd have been too embarrassed. Pride was as important to Matt as it would be to anybody.

"Well?" Laney prompted. "You didn't answer my question."

James knew it was now or never. He might not have told people he was gay, but he'd never lied about his sexuality either. He didn't want to start now.

"Yes," he replied, finally finding the strength from somewhere within to say the words out loud. "I'm gay."

A loud gasp caught both his and Laney's attention and when James' head automatically turned to the sound, he saw his mother standing at the door, eyes wide in disbelief. Her slim, elegant hand was covering her mouth. James' stomach lurched. Well that sure settled the argument with Maria about whether or not his mother knew. He got up from his chair and crossed the room until he was standing in front of his mother.

"Mom?"

His mother dropped her hand and turned to Matt, who stood next to her holding what looked like some sort of pie. "I can't stay or I'll be late for my shift at the hospital," she said. "But I just wanted to bring you something to make sure you were eating."

"Uh, this was really great of you," Matt said somewhat awkwardly. "I appreciate you thinking of me."

James' mother waved off Matt's gratitude and turned to leave. She paused on her way back to the front door. "Will you let me know when the funeral is?"

"Of course," Matt replied.

She nodded and let herself out of the door without so much as a glance in James' direction. He scrubbed a hand over his face then met Matt's gaze. "You think I should go after her?"

"I don't know. Maybe it would be best to give her some time. Let her calm down."

James nodded. "Right."

"So, you're not actually out?" Matt asked. There was something that looked like disappointment in his eyes. "Not to anyone?"

"No," James answered quietly. "I'm not out."

"Well, at least she didn't rant and rave," Laney said. "That has to count for something, right?"

"I think I would have preferred it if she had. To just say nothing?" James shook his head. "She's been mad at me a hundred or more times, but she's never ignored me like that, not ever."

Matt put the pie down on the kitchen counter then placed a comforting hand on James' shoulder. "She'll come around," he said.

James tried to smile, but he was afraid it came out as more of a grimace. Matt knew better than anyone that wasn't always the case. Sometimes people took their hurt and anger to the grave. He hoped that wouldn't be the case with his mother. He couldn't bear that.

"Yeah," he replied, trying to inject as much optimism into his voice as possible. "She'll come around."

* * * *

Matt parked his sedan next to James' car and killed the engine. He still couldn't believe he'd agreed to meet James at their spot by the river. Was he insane? Just what the hell did he think he was doing? This couldn't lead to anything good, but Matt hadn't been able to turn James down when he had asked. Just like when they were kids he was willing to do whatever the hell James wanted, no questions asked. His head was filled with James. Matt wasn't sure what bothered him more, that James was the first face in his mind's eye when he woke up in the morning, or that he wished it was James' actual face he saw when he awoke. Either scenario could only lead to heartbreak.

He locked the car and followed the familiar path through the trees until he reached the clearing. James was already there. He had a red-checked blanket spread out on the ground near their rock and a delicious-looking picnic lay in the middle. It looked wonderful, but Matt couldn't work out why James was trying so hard. What did he hope to achieve? Was this an innocent step towards rebuilding their friendship or was this James' way of seducing him? Even as the thought entered his head it sent a shiver of anticipation down Matt's spine. Did he want to be seduced by James? Hell yeah. Even though he knew he shouldn't.

"Hey, you made it." James stood up and rubbed his hands down the front of his jeans and Matt was able to get a good look at him. James was dressed in a plain grey T-shirt and dark denims that fit snugly over his hips. He looked hotter than sin and Matt knew that was without even trying. His light-blond hair was cut just long enough to frame eyes the colour of the ocean on a clear day. Matt's breathing came faster and his heart sped up in his chest.

"I got Angela to cover at the diner for me and I made us lunch," James said, motioning to the spread laid out before them. "I thought you might like to get out of the house and enjoy the sunshine for a while."

Matt chewed on his bottom lip, feeling suddenly incredibly nervous. "Uh, thanks. You shouldn't have gone to so much trouble."

"It was no trouble. Come, sit down."

Matt hesitated for a few seconds until he saw the look of nervous expectation on James' face, which no doubt mirrored his own, and decided to put him out of his misery. He took a seat on the blanket and looked at all the food set out in front of him so that he wouldn't have to look in those eyes that had the power to see right into his very soul, or so it seemed.

"This looks great," he said, pointing at the selection of meats, cheeses and crusty bread. Right on cue, Matt's stomach grumbled loudly and James chuckled.

Reaching into a small cooler, James retrieved a can of soda and handed it to Matt. They were quiet while they ate but it was a companionable silence — it didn't feel awkward in any way. The food, the heat from the sunshine and the gentle sound of the water running past them went some way towards alleviating Matt's nerves. He closed his eyes and leaned his head back, enjoying the heat of the sun as it warmed his face. It had been a long time since he'd done this.

When he opened his eyes, he caught James staring at him and just like that the spell was broken. Matt looked away quickly. What had he seen in James' eyes that made him feel so damn nervous all of a sudden? He and James had grown up together and Matt had never felt anything but completely comfortable with him before. Conversation had come easily — hell, just being together had been easy — but this, this was different. This was something new and Matt didn't have a clue how to handle it. So he handled it the only way he knew how — he became antagonistic.

"Why did you do all this, James? What did you hope to gain?"

James brushed the crumbs off his hands and frowned. "I didn't hope to gain anything. I just wanted to do something nice for you."

"But what do *you* get out of it?"

James smiled wryly. "It was supposed to be the pleasure of your company, but that was before you decided to be a dick."

Matt sat up straighter and glared at James. He knew he was behaving like a spoilt brat, but now that he'd started down this track he didn't know how to stop himself. And the anger was easier to deal with than the hurt and the grief—at least that's what he told himself when he questioned James' motives. "I'm not falling for that. What do you want from me?"

James scowled. "What do you think I want, huh? What do *you* think this is all about, Matt? Come on, you must have some idea in that thick head of yours or you wouldn't have brought it up."

"Okay. I think you're trying to seduce me."

James looked taken aback for a moment then he threw his head back and laughed. When he next met Matt's gaze his shoulders were still shaking. "That's it? That's what you came up with? You think this is all some elaborate plot so that I can get my leg over?"

Matt felt his cheeks fill with heat. "Well, how the hell do I know what you want?"

James sighed. "Wow. I must have hurt you pretty badly if that's all you think of me, huh?"

"I got over it," Matt lied.

All of the fight seemed to go out of James and he hunched forward and stared at his wrung hands. "I'm glad," he said quietly. "I wish you never had to get over anything. I wish I never hurt you in the first place. I'm sorry, Matt. I'll tell you every day until you believe me."

Matt could see nothing but truth in James' eyes when he

looked up at him, and it made him fold in on himself, his incomprehensible need for combat ended by James' words. This wasn't a competition to see who could get one up on the other, it wasn't a battle and James hadn't brought him here for anything other than an attempt at reconciliation. It was up to Matt if he wanted to accept James' olive branch.

Matt knew he was at a crossroads and there were only two paths he could choose — forgive James and have the friend back that he'd missed so much over the years, or get up and walk away. He didn't ever have to see James again if he didn't want to. But even the thought of never seeing him again caused an almighty ache in his chest. Yes, James had hurt him when they were eighteen, and hurt him badly, but how long could he keep making him suffer for what he'd done?

Maybe it really was time to forgive and forget. If he didn't then he hadn't learnt anything from his father's death, had he? How much would he love a chance to make things right with his pop? It was too late for that, but it wasn't too late for James. Matt leaned across the blanket and placed a tentative hand on James' shoulder.

"You never have to say you're sorry for that again. It was ten years ago — a long time. I forgive you and I think it's about time for me to forget what happened too. Time for both of us to forget."

"You mean that?" The hope that surged in James' eyes brought a lump to Matt's throat and tears began to form but he kept them hidden.

"Every word."

A wide grin tugged at James' lips and the expression warmed Matt's heart and lifted his spirits until he too was grinning, his heart feeling suddenly lighter.

"Let's go for a swim," James said, looking down into the water.

"You've got to be kidding me."

James laughed. "No, I'm not kidding. Come on, for old times' sake."

Matt shook his head. "I haven't got anything to wear."

James wiggled his eyebrows but stayed silent and Matt laughed.

"Naked?"

"Is there any other way to swim in the river?"

Matt shrugged. "I guess not."

Within minutes they had stripped off all their clothes and had jumped in. Matt tried his best not to look at James' body as he got naked and waded in before him, but the perfect view he got of his firm ass caused a low moan to rip from his throat.

James must have heard because he turned and asked, "Everything okay?"

"It's cold," Matt replied, thinking on his feet. The water *was* cold at first and caused gooseflesh to rise on his arms, but he acclimatised quickly and soon he was racing James to the other side of the bank.

They swam and frolicked for another twenty minutes, splashing each other and dunking each other's heads. It was the most fun Matt had had in a long time. But when a sharp rock on the riverbed dug into his foot and made him yelp, they both made their way back to the riverbank where their clothes waited for them. James was first out of the water.

"Let's dry off on our rock before we put our clothes back on," he suggested.

Matt nodded and followed him in his wake. He liked that James had called it 'our rock'. They stretched out side by side just as they had done dozens of times in their youth and closed their eyes, enjoying the warmth of the sun on their bare skin.

"Mmm, I missed being here and relaxing in the sun," Matt commented idly.

James sighed. "Me too."

Matt opened his eyes at that comment and turned to face James. "What do you mean? Didn't you ever come out here in the last ten years?"

James shook his head. "Never. I couldn't face seeing the place when you were gone. Besides, it wouldn't have been the same without you."

Matt didn't know what to say to that so he didn't say anything. There was nothing he could say that would have sounded right anyway.

"I didn't just miss this, you know — lying here in the sun, I mean. I missed doing it with you."

When Matt turned his head again, James was looking his way, his head just inches away, their lips within kissing distance. Matt forgot how to breathe. He'd have turned away, but James' eyes were locked onto his own, holding him there like the most powerful magnet. And then it was James who was leaning forward and closing the distance between them until their lips met. The kiss was soft at first, the faintest brush of soft flesh against flesh, but then James pressed harder, his tongue appearing between them and sliding against Matt's lips, asking to be let in. Matt could do nothing but open up and invite James inside.

James fisted his hand in Matt's hair and pulled him closer as he deepened the kiss, his tongue doing things to his mouth that should be illegal. It was the hottest, sweetest, most perfect damn kiss Matt had ever known. When James finally pulled back to lay his forehead against Matt's, he was breathing heavily.

"That should have been our first kiss when we were eighteen," James whispered against Matt's lips. "That was exactly how it felt for me the first time, but I got scared."

Matt shook his head. "I told you, you don't need to apologise to me again."

"I'm not, but I'd like to explain." James took his hand from Matt's head and moved back, widening the distance between their bodies. He looked down and Matt couldn't help but follow his gaze until he was looking at James' hard cock sitting proudly against his hip. Matt groaned.

"You see what you do to me?" James asked, smiling almost shyly. "The same damn thing happened the first time you kissed me and it scared the living shit out of me. I was convinced the kiss was just a spur-of-the-moment thing for you. I thought you'd regret it as soon as you came to your senses and then you'd look down and see how hard the kiss made me and you'd know I was gay.

"I thought you'd think there was something wrong with me. So I lashed out before that could happen." James sighed. "I was stupid. A damn fool. But the worst thing I did was not swallowing my pride and apologising to you later. I should have explained all this ten years ago and then maybe we wouldn't have wasted so much time."

"The important thing is that we don't waste any more time," Matt said. "If this is what we both want then...I'd like to see where things go between us."

James looked up and met Matt's gaze and a smile tugged the corner of his lips. "Do you have any idea how happy you just made me?"

Matt grinned and his gaze slid down James' body to come to rest on his rather impressive erection. "Is that a trick question?"

James raised an amused eyebrow. "Seal the deal with a kiss?"

"God yes."

The second time their mouths came together, the kiss was more frantic than the first—a blur of teeth and tongue and a battle for dominance that left Matt full of need, his cock aching between his legs. Their chests pressed together first, then stomachs met and then—oh sweet God—their hard, insistent cocks rubbed against each other deliciously. Matt gasped into the kiss, his hands coming up to fist in James' hair.

"Jesus, touch me, James. Please."

James growled and pushed Matt over until he lay flat on his back, James' lean, hard body covering his. The weight of him felt just right. Water dripped down from James' hair, but Matt ignored it and concentrated instead on the stunning blue eyes that were looking deeply into his. James reached a hand between them and slid it around Matt's cock, his thumb brushing over the sensitive nerve endings under the head, and Matt slammed his head back against the rock, his back arching, all the breath in his lungs gone.

"Oh God," Matt breathed. "More."

James made a strangled-sounding moan and tightened his fist around Matt's cock. Just when Matt thought he would go out of his head with need, James started stroking, keeping the firm grip that Matt liked so damn much. Matt slid his hands around James' hips, his fingers biting into flesh, clutching hard enough to leave a mark.

"James!" Matt was close, right on the edge of coming. Another couple of strokes would be all it took. But he wanted James there with him when he fell into the abyss.

With much effort, Matt removed one of his hands from James' hip and brought it between them, his fingers tangling with James' as he reached for his cock. James let out a low hiss as soon as Matt's fingers came into contact with his hard length, then James' grip tightened when he threw his head back and wailed out Matt's name. Matt felt the warm, wet evidence of James' release on his hand and stomach and it pushed him over the edge. James' tugs grew erratic with his own release, but it didn't matter, Matt was already there. As the sensations overwhelmed his body, he let out a choking sob, clenched every muscle in his body and came—hard and spectacularly.

James grunted and fell forward, his hands braced on the rock, on either side of Matt's head. Despite his look of sated exhaustion there was laughter in his eyes. "Or we could seal the deal with a hand job," he joked.

Matt shook his head. "What am I going to do with you?"

"Whatever you want," James replied easily.

Chapter Six

"This is Lizzie, she likes chocolate," Hope said, straightening out the ballgown on a much played with Barbie. She thrust the doll at Matt and picked up another.

James turned to gauge Matt's reaction. He had a bemused look on his face, but James couldn't blame him. Both of James' sisters had kids, so he'd had several years to get used to children and their tireless games, but Matt had been thrown in at the deep end. Despite being way out of his element he was taking Hope's unwavering attention in his stride.

"Does she?" Matt asked. "I hope you've told her too much chocolate is bad for her."

Hope cocked her head to the side. "I tried, but I don't think she believes me," she said in the high-pitched voice James had always found endearing. "Maybe if *you* told her."

James chuckled as Matt lifted the doll and waggled his finger in front of its face. "If you eat any more chocolate and lose that smoking body of yours, you're going to regret it," he said.

Hope giggled and James snorted, nearly choking on his pretend cup of tea.

"Should it bother me you're noticing the figure of a female doll?"

Matt grinned. "Anything to keep you on your toes."

It was good to see Matt smile. James knew how much losing his father was weighing on Matt and, although he was putting on a brave face, he had to be hurting. Matt and his father had had a good relationship once, right up until the time Hank had lost his wife. Matt's mom had been a warm, caring woman who was full of love. It flowed out of her every pore, consuming everything in its path. You couldn't help but feel good around her, like you knew you were in the presence of someone special. Hank never did recover from her death. It seemed he didn't know how to cope without her and had no interest in learning how.

The funeral was taking place in three days. James had been doing his best to keep Matt occupied in the week up until the big day so he wouldn't dwell on what was coming. Maria had gone on another date and James had roped Matt into babysitting with him, although from the look on his face he didn't seem to mind at all. While Hope was rummaging through her toy chest trying to find a new outfit for one of her dolls, James reached out and put a hand on Matt's knee.

"You're good with kids," he said, nodding to Hope. "You ever think about having any of your own?"

Matt shrugged. "Not really. I like kids. I just never thought I'd get the opportunity. You?"

"Same, I guess. Providence is not exactly the type of place you could adopt and raise kids, you know?"

"Why not? It's as good a place as any."

James snorted. "You haven't lived here in the past ten years."

Matt furrowed his brow. "What do you mean? What's wrong with it here?"

James chose his words carefully. "There's nothing wrong with it, exactly. There are just some people that wouldn't approve, and they'd be very vocal about it too. Could make life difficult."

Matt gave him a wry smile. "And it's obvious *you* haven't lived anywhere but Providence for any length of time. Those people are everywhere, James. There are always going to be people who don't approve of what you do. There's no escaping them. They're in every town and every country." Matt shrugged. "It's up to you if you choose to pay attention to them or not. I never did."

"You make it sound so easy."

"It's not. But then, nothing that's worth anything in life comes easy."

"You sound like one of those positive thinking gurus. There something I should know about you?" James teased.

Matt turned his face away quickly, but not before James saw the hint of a blush spread across his cheeks.

"Oh God. Please don't tell me I'm dating one of those. I don't think I could stand to be woken up at stupid o'clock in the morning to do a hundred press-ups and then go for a ten-mile run."

"Shut up," Matt chastised. "I'm not *that* bad. I just might have taken a positive thinking course. Or two."

James threw his head back and laughed. "Oh, God help me. He's going to try and convert me to the dark side."

Matt grinned. "There are worse things than having a positive outlook on life, you know."

"I'm sure," James replied, still smiling. "I just can't think of any right now."

Matt shook his head, but just like James had planned, he had a smile on his face a mile wide. God, he loved to see Matt smile. He'd give anything to keep the expression on Matt's lips, anything at all.

"Are you gay?" Hope asked Matt.

The question evidently caught Matt off guard because he shot a panicked look at James, who had to fight to suppress his mirth. He knew he should help Matt out, but this was too much fun. He loved that a five-year-old had the ability to render Matt speechless.

"Mommy said that Uncle James is gay because he's happy and he likes to play with men," Hope clarified.

"Uh, well, if that's the criteria, I guess that makes me gay, too," Matt replied.

Hope nodded solemnly. "I thought so."

James did laugh at Matt's raised eyebrows then — he couldn't stop himself and it only took a moment before Matt joined in, chuckling and shaking his head. Hope was oblivious. She was busy pulling books and pens out of her trunk.

"Can we colour now?" she asked, holding up a book.

James grinned. "Why don't you ask Uncle Matt? Colouring is his *favourite* thing."

Matt grabbed the book from Hope and patted the seat next to him for her to sit down. He didn't say anything, but shot James a look that told him he was going to pay for that remark.

An hour later, after many loud protests and a few tears, James managed to put Hope to bed. He was exhausted. He could understand why Maria was always so tired. He wouldn't change Hope for anything, and he doubted Maria would either, but damn—five-year-olds were hard work. When he walked back into the living room, it looked as though a bomb had gone off in there. Matt was on his hands and knees picking up jigsaw pieces.

"Hey, you didn't have to clean up," he said, kneeling beside Matt and helping to pick up the pieces. "I could have done it."

Matt shrugged. "It's no trouble. Gave me something to do."

"I think I finally got her to go to sleep."

Matt shook his head, a small smile playing on his lips. "She certainly is a handful. I don't know how Maria copes with her full-time."

"Me either." James chuckled. "I don't think even Maria knows how she does it. But I'd assume there's caffeine involved. Lots and lots of caffeine."

Matt snorted. "No doubt."

When they'd finished clearing up the room, James put a large pepperoni pizza in the oven. They ate it while they watched a new action flick James had rented especially for the night. It felt good to spend time with Matt again. After the pizza, they sat side by side on the sofa, legs pressed against each other, and James' arm was flung over Matt's shoulder. The smell of Matt's cologne was a pleasant distraction and on more than one occasion James found himself leaning in closer and inhaling the spicy scent. Matt didn't seem to notice and, if he did, he didn't appear to mind. As the movie progressed, he too moved closer to James' side. It was good that Matt felt comfortable with him again. It had been beyond James' wildest imaginings that he would become friends with Matt again, let alone anything more. He couldn't have been happier.

The heat from where Matt's leg was pressed against his was starting to affect James in ways he didn't want to be thinking about when he was babysitting Hope. But it was all he *could* think about when Matt's hand found his knee and his fingers started stroking lazy circles and slowly moving upwards. James could feel the gentle touch even through the thick material of his jeans and it was driving him insane. He finally gave up all pretence of watching the movie and grabbed Matt's head, pulling him closer until their lips found each other and his tongue pushed into the warm, wet confines of Matt's mouth. Matt groaned and opened up for him and pretty soon they were hot and heavy — hips thrusting and limbs tangled together.

"What was that?" Matt asked, pulling away from James' mouth just enough for the words to be coherent.

"Huh?"

Matt shook his head. "Just thought I heard something, that's all."

"Was nothing," James mumbled, recapturing Matt's lips and sliding his hand down Matt's taut abdomen.

The clearing of a throat near the door brought James to his senses and when he pulled back from Matt's mouth and looked across the room he saw his sister standing with her arms folded and an amused expression on her face. John Delucca stood next to her. James yelped and pushed Matt away. He got to his feet and ran a hand through his hair.

"Uh, you're home."

Maria rolled her eyes. "Nope, I'm just a figment of your overactive imagination. Yes, I'm home. Idiot." Maria turned to John and nodded to James. "John, you remember my brother, and Matt Jacobs, from school?"

"Uh, hi guys," John said, smiling at James and Matt in turn. "It's been a while."

John was shorter than James' sister and more rotund. He was only twenty-six, the same age as Maria, but already his fine, dark hair was starting to recede. He was the polar opposite to Maria's ex. In fact, he was completely different from anyone James had seen his sister date in the past. Which wasn't a bad thing. Her usual choice in men sucked.

"Hi, John," Matt said, stepping forward and shaking John's hand. "Good to see you again."

"You too. And I was sorry to hear about your father. He was a good man. Taught me everything I know. I'll be taking the time off to go to the funeral, of course."

"Thanks. You still working at his old practice?"

John nodded. "Yeah, I bought the practice myself, matter of fact, a couple of years ago now."

"Oh, I didn't realise."

James had forgotten that John had worked in the same practice as Hank before he'd retired.

"Hank sold the practice to Bob Weaver, but his family moved out of state and I was interested. So..." He shrugged.

"Well, congratulations," Matt said. "I hope you'll be as happy there as my pop was."

"Thanks. Are you back home for good now?"

Matt looked at James before he answered, "Yeah, I think so."

"I'm glad. Maria tells me you bought a diner, James," John said.

"Uh, yeah, yeah I did." James looked to his sister in the hope she'd put him out of his misery, but he was sorely mistaken. She and Matt were handling the situation far better than he was. James just wanted the ground to open up and swallow him where he stood. He'd never been so embarrassed. But then, Matt had been out for years and Maria didn't have an ounce of shame in her body. She didn't get embarrassed...ever.

"Right, well, I've got an early start tomorrow so I'd better get going," James said. "Matt?"

Matt cocked his head and regarded James strangely. "Uh, sure—okay. I suppose I'll see you soon, Maria. John, it was good to see you again. I guess I'll see you at the funeral."

James headed for the door.

"Uh, James, have you forgotten something?" Maria asked.

James spun around and stared at his sister. "What did I forget?"

Maria raised an amused eyebrow. "You remember that annoying five-year-old that flies around like a tornado, creating havoc in her path. Calls you Uncle James?"

"Hope!" James exclaimed.

"That'd be the one."

Thankfully, Matt answered for James. "She was good as gold. We played with just about every doll and game in her toy chest and we fed her too much cake. She finally crashed out after her sugar rush."

Maria laughed. "Perfect. Well, goodnight then. You'd better watch yourself, Matt. I might call on you again."

Matt gave a slight bow. "Anytime I can be of service, m'lady."

After they'd said their goodbyes, Matt put a hand on James' lower back and led him to the front door. He waited until they were in the car before speaking.

"Wow, you were a nervous wreck in there. What was that all about?"

James let out a long breath. "We just got caught kissing. My hand was down your pants."

Matt chuckled. "So it was. Felt good, too."

James scowled. "Doesn't it bother you at all, people knowing?"

Now it was Matt's turn to scowl. "Why the hell should it? I've got nothing to be ashamed of. We weren't doing anything wrong back there. It was just a kiss."

"Guess so," James mumbled.

They didn't talk for the rest of the drive back to Matt's house and, even though he didn't say anything, James got the impression that Matt was angry with him, or at least upset by his reaction. He wished he could be as open as Matt was, but he didn't know how. He'd been hiding that part of himself for so long it felt natural to do so. And he still wasn't even convinced he wanted everyone to know about his sexuality or his relationship with Matt. What would they gain by everyone knowing, and whose business was it really but theirs?

When James turned to look at Matt, he felt incredibly ashamed of himself. If he hadn't been so intent on hiding the person he was all those years ago and if he hadn't been such a coward—just as he'd been tonight—he wouldn't have lost the most important person in his life. His actions had cost him ten years without Matt at his side. If he didn't man up, James feared the separation would be much longer the next time, probably forever. He couldn't let that happen. If he wanted his relationship with Matt to work, he had to fight for it.

* * * *

Matt closed the front door and leaned his forehead against the glass panel while he tried to gather his thoughts. It had been a long couple of days. News of his father's death had circulated around town and his father's friends and acquaintances had dropped by in droves to pay their condolences. Matt hadn't understood how news had got around so quickly until Laney had told him she and her mom had been informing as many of Hank's friends as they could think of. His pop's lawyer had probably told some people too. Matt had known the job had to be done, but he hadn't been looking forward to doing it, so he was grateful Laney had taken it upon herself to make a lot of the calls for him.

They'd put their heads together to work out if there was

anyone left who needed to be told and Matt had dutifully made the rest of the phone calls. Each call was harder than the last. Matt wasn't sure how many more times he could listen to someone telling him how sorry they were. Planning a funeral was exhausting. Matt had no idea there would be so much involved, but actually he was glad of it. Keeping himself busy was the best way to keep his mind off his dad's passing. And there was a lot to be done.

Matt had to admit James had been wonderful throughout the entire ordeal. He couldn't have asked for a better set of friends at his side. Neither Matt nor Laney had planned a funeral before, so James had taken the helm. It seemed the funeral director would take care of most of the arrangements, but there were other things to consider too, like the wake. That was the thing Matt was least looking forward to. Standing around talking to a bunch of near strangers after he'd just buried his father was going to be tough, for sure, but there was no avoiding it.

"How are you feeling?" James stepped up behind Matt and placed a hand on his shoulder.

Matt shrugged. "Holding up, I guess."

James nodded and gave Matt's shoulder a quick squeeze. "You're doing good, Matt, you're doing real good."

Matt turned and met James' gaze and his stomach jolted when their eyes locked. He was getting used to having James around and their renewed friendship was going from strength to strength, but Matt couldn't help but feel he was setting himself up for a fall. James had made it clear he wanted a relationship with Matt, but the main problem was that James still wasn't out. What sort of relationship would they have? Sure, James' mom had known for a couple of days now, but that hadn't been through choice. His sister knew, too, and now John, but it seemed James had no intention of letting his sexual preference become common knowledge. If they were to embark on a serious relationship then James' decisions would affect Matt too.

Hadn't Matt just been through the same thing with Tom?

He didn't know if he could go through a secret relationship again. Would he constantly have to hide his feelings for James? Could he ever hold his hand in public or place a kiss on his cheek? What about something as simple as a dinner date? Would James mind dining in a restaurant with him or would that be too intimate? The questions were endless and went round and round in Matt's head until he felt dizzy from them. He had to know where he stood.

He brushed past James and strode into the living room. He waited for James to follow then turned to face him.

"I've been thinking."

James grinned. "Wonders will never cease."

"Smartass. What do you say we go for a meal in that new Italian one day after the funeral? Laney said the food there is really good."

James' smile was bright. It was the sort of smile you couldn't fake. "Sounds great, count me in."

"Uh, I meant just you and I."

James furrowed his brow. "That's what I thought you meant."

Damn. Maybe Matt was worrying over nothing. Besides, James wasn't Tom. There was a world of difference between them. James crossed the room and slid his arms around Matt's waist. That was another thing Matt was getting used to—James touching him. It was becoming as familiar to him as breathing. It was usually just a pat on the shoulder or a casual touch to his arm, sometimes a reassuring hand on his lower back, but when it was something tender and far more affectionate it sent shivers through Matt's body and made him want to moan from the pleasure of it all.

James leaned in close and brushed their lips together and the moan he'd been trying to hold in escaped his lips. He could feel James smile against his mouth then his tongue appeared and traced the seam of Matt's lips. Just a few days ago Matt would have resisted, but now he needed James' kisses like he needed air. He opened his mouth and sighed when James slipped his tongue inside his mouth.

James pulled him closer, grinding his hips into Matt's with an almost desperate need. Matt didn't know who moaned the loudest. He didn't care. While they writhed against one another and the kiss became more urgent, Matt couldn't think of anything but the burning desire to come and to make James come too. It was a need that overrode every other...a compulsion, even. He wanted to be the man responsible for making James fly apart. But just like every other time they'd kissed since the time by the lake, James pulled back. Matt wasn't sure what was holding James back, but he hadn't been as carefree since John and Maria had caught them kissing the other night.

"I think we should stop," James said breathlessly. "I should go home before this gets out of hand."

Just the idea of James leaving made Matt's chest feel tight. "Is that what you want?" he rasped.

"Hell no! But it doesn't matter what I want — it's the right thing to do."

Matt's gaze fell to James' kiss-swollen lips as James flicked his tongue out to wet them. Matt licked his own. He was tired of holding back, tired of denying what he so desperately wanted, what they both wanted. His hands came up and fisted in James' hair and he took his mouth, forcing his tongue inside, making James gasp. This time Matt was the one to pull back, but it was only so he could trace his tongue along James' neck and nip the lobe of his ear.

"I say we forget about doing the right thing and do what we both want," he whispered into James' ear.

James sighed and pulled back. He took a long moment to stare into Matt's eyes, but he must have finally seen what he wanted there because he said, "Give me a couple of minutes. I need to get something from the car."

Matt's heart started beating faster. "Please tell me you're getting condoms and lube."

James smiled and nodded. "I picked some up from the drugstore yesterday, but I didn't want to be so presumptuous as to bring them in with me."

Matt had considered buying some himself, but the stupid part of his brain had told him they didn't need them yet. It was too soon. Now he couldn't understand why the hell he'd listened to that voice — the timing was perfect.

"Hurry back," he said against James' lips.

While James went out to the car, Matt ran around the house switching off lights and making sure the windows were locked. By the time he had finished, James was waiting for him right where he'd left him. The heat and intensity in James' eyes were almost enough to make him blush.

"Let's go upstairs." He reached for James' free hand with the intention of tugging him along, but instead James pulled him close to his body, his arms circling Matt's waist.

"Tell me one last time this is what you want and I won't ask again," James said.

Matt placed a chaste kiss against James' lips and rubbed his still rock-hard cock against the front of James' jeans to leave him with no doubt this was what he wanted.

James let out a low moan. "Take me to your bed, Matt."

Matt didn't hesitate. He grabbed hold of James' hand and pulled him along and they eventually made it upstairs to his bedroom. They had to keep stopping on the way because James would grope Matt's ass or pull him back for a kiss that was probably only intended to be quick, but as soon as their mouths came together they were loath to separate for even a single second.

Inside Matt's bedroom, James placed the condoms and lube on the nightstand and kicked off his shoes. Matt did the same. No other item of clothing was removed before James grabbed hold of Matt's hips and pulled him hard against his body. He trailed kisses down Matt's neck, his tongue flicking out to tease against the sensitive skin and, as James' breath warmed Matt's neck, he slipped his fingers into Matt's hair and held on tight.

James nipped Matt's neck and Matt let out a low, breathless moan. When James pulled back, there was a devilish smile on his lips. A firm hand found its way to Matt's straining erection and squeezed and Matt gasped, bucking into the touch, wanting more.

"Imagine how that's going to feel when we're naked," James whispered in his ear. "My hand on your bare cock. Just like last time."

Matt groaned. "Jesus. Can we get naked? Like now?"

James chuckled and grabbed the bottom of Matt's T-shirt, lifting it in one smooth movement up Matt's body and over his head and arms. Then he removed his own shirt and Matt got lost for a moment on the contours of James' muscular chest and flat, lean stomach. A fine dusting of hair covered his torso, leading to the prize.

"God, you're beautiful," Matt breathed. "I think I could get off just looking at you."

James burst out laughing. "I hope not. I was planning on getting laid tonight."

Matt laughed too—relieved at the lightness of spirit he felt when he was with James. Being with him didn't feel awkward in any way. It was as though it was meant to be. That was a nice idea.

He liked to believe there was someone out there for everyone and that James belonged to him and only him. But he didn't dare tell James that—he had a feeling James would just roll his eyes and joke about him being sentimental. James slid his hands down Matt's chest and stomach until he reached the buckle of his belt. He undid it deftly and slid Matt's pants down his hips. That was a good thing because there didn't appear to be enough space in them anymore to accommodate Matt's swollen cock.

With only his briefs covering his erection, James' hand stroking over the material felt incredible. His cock felt even more sensitive than before. James leant forward and covered his mouth and Matt whimpered into the kiss. When James' tongue entered his mouth and danced with his own, Matt returned the kiss with fervour. Teeth knocked together as their tongues fought for dominance and all the while James stroked every inch of exposed skin he could reach.

When the need to breathe overrode desire, James pulled back and nipped the delicate skin just below Matt's ear. Matt could do nothing but hold on for the ride. He couldn't seem to keep his hands off James either, wanting to touch him everywhere at once. James' mouth travelled lower down his throat and across his chest until he took a nipple in his mouth. Matt could barely think straight. He hadn't even realised they were moving backwards until his legs bumped against the base of the bed.

James' mouth continued its exploration of Matt's body. From one nipple to the next, he moved lower, his tongue flicking out to lick a path down Matt's stomach, until his mouth closed over the tip of his erection, which was poking out of the top of his briefs. Matt cried out. The wet heat of James' mouth on the head of his cock sent shivers racing over his body. It was almost too much...almost.

Matt's hips jerked forward involuntarily, seeking out more of the heat of James' mouth. The need to thrust forward until James took him deeper was intense, but Matt held back and let James move at his own pace. It took all of his willpower, but he managed to keep still as James' hot tongue dipped into his slit, driving him crazy with need.

"Let's get the rest of these clothes off you, yeah?" James said when he pulled back.

Thank God. James' mouth sliding over the head of his cock felt amazing, but Matt needed more. He needed James naked, on top of him...in him.

They each removed their own clothes. Matt didn't think he'd be able to take the distraction of having his hands on James and from the look on his face, James felt the same way. It didn't take them long until they stood in front of each other naked. James' gaze raked down Matt's body like a caress. It was as though he was memorising every inch of him.

"Stunning," said James, reaching out to stroke his fingers lightly down Matt's side.

It was too much for Matt. He reached out and grabbed James and tugged him close, slanting his mouth over James' and pushing his tongue inside forcefully. James' body slammed into his, knocking him backwards until they were lying on the bed, limbs tangled together. The kisses were hot and demanding, filled with the need of two people who had wanted each other for too long a time. Matt had never felt so needy or needed, but the way James kissed him left no doubt how much he desired him. It was an exciting thought. They writhed against one another while they kissed, hands learning each other's body while their lips and tongues learnt every inch of each other's mouth. Matt couldn't remember ever being this excited or ever wanting someone the way he wanted James. His need for the man lying above him, grinding into him, was all-consuming.

Matt couldn't remember who finally reached for the bottle of lube. He didn't know whose idea it was to lift his legs towards his chest and have James' fingers enter him, but it was a damn good one. Sweat dripped down Matt's forehead as James stroked him in his most intimate place. Matt wanted to cry out from the sheer joy of it, but James was keeping his mouth busy while he worked his fingers. He stole his breath with kisses that should be illegal they were so good. And then James hit that spot inside him that left him with no option but to pull away from James' mouth and shout out his pleasure.

"Yes!"

James growled in his ear. "Jesus, tell me you're nearly ready, 'cause I'm about ready to blow here."

Matt laughed and nodded. "Never been more ready. Fuck me, James."

The next thing Matt knew, James' fingers disappeared and Matt was too damn empty. He whimpered and arched his back, lifted his ass and begged with his body for James to fill him, to take him. He grabbed his legs behind his knees and lifted them closer to his chest.

The cold, wet slickness of lube-covered fingers slid over

his entrance one last time before he heard the rip of foil then James' cock was nudging at his entrance, asking to be let in. Matt tried to relax both his body and his mind as James' cock pushed past the first point of resistance. It smarted a little, but soon James was deeper inside and the sting lessened.

"Jesus Christ, so good, so damn good," James was babbling, sweat dripping from his forehead as he pressed in farther. His arms were shaking from the control he was exerting, but all the while his eyes never left Matt's.

"You okay?" he panted. "I'm not hurting you?"

"Hell no, you're not. It feels great."

James nodded and kept pushing forward inch by inch until he finally bottomed out. He leant forward and grinned—his eyes filled with desire. Matt was reminded of a predator that had just caught his prey and the image made him shiver.

They stayed perfectly still until they both had time to adjust to the sensation, then James' eyebrows rose in query.

Matt nodded. "Do it."

James didn't need to be told twice. He slid out slowly and slammed back inside. Matt clutched at the sheets, desperately reaching for something to keep him grounded as James thrust into him again and again with increasing speed and urgency, threatening to make him fly apart. James wrapped his arms around Matt's legs, holding on as he thrust inside. Then he shifted his weight on the mattress and the new position made him enter at a different angle until he was deeper than before and grazing Matt's prostate with every pass.

There was a lot of noise in the room. Both men were groaning and grunting and the old metal bed was creaking ominously in accompaniment. With every breath Matt took, the sweet scent of sweat and sex filled his nostrils until he was nearly dizzy from it. And underneath, the aroma of James, of his cologne, permeated Matt's senses filling him with delight.

James set up a brutal rhythm, fucking Matt in earnest until Matt didn't know which way was up. Every time James nailed his prostate, Matt shouted his pleasure to the heavens. Then as though James were reading his mind, a hand encircled his cock and began to stroke and Matt knew it was all over.

"James! I... Argh!"

After just two more tugs of his cock, Matt slammed his head back into the pillow and came. He was dimly aware of James shouting out his name, his thrusts becoming erratic and frenzied as he, too, achieved his release and came inside Matt, filling the condom with his seed. James released Matt's legs and leaned over him, stealing a kiss and all the breath he had left in his lungs. Matt had never felt so boneless, or so sated or so completely right. As James finally released his mouth and collapsed on top of him, Matt wondered absently how he'd managed for ten years without this wonderful feeling — without James.

"Jesus," James said, bracing his arms on either side of Matt's head. "That was incredible. Better than the fantasy."

Matt smiled. "You fantasised about me?"

James' cheeks filled with colour. "Only every damn night since I was a teenager."

"Oh," Matt said, stroking his hand down James' cheek. "Not much then."

James chuckled and pressed a quick kiss to his lips. "No. Not much at all."

Chapter Seven

Matt barely had time to blink before the day of the funeral arrived, but he didn't know if that was a good thing or not. On the one hand he was glad he could finally put his pop to rest and say a last goodbye to him, but he was in no way prepared to do it. James, Maria and Laney had seen to it he hadn't been alone for more than an hour in the days leading up to the funeral, and he couldn't express his gratitude enough. Matt didn't know for sure, but he suspected James and his sister had got together with Laney behind his back and arranged it that way. He was glad if they had. He didn't know how he would have coped alone, but he suspected he wouldn't have done very well at all.

The only time he'd had to himself was bedtime, and even then he'd had difficulty saying goodnight to James — who'd had a hell of a lot more willpower than Matt had. James was always the one to end their heated goodbye kisses before they reached the point of no return. Matt hadn't expected that, but James was full of surprises. After they'd had sex for the first time, Matt had thought the momentum would continue, but James had always been the more sensible of the two. He'd said it would be better for them to slow things down — at least until after the funeral when Matt had had some time to come to terms with his grief.

Matt thought he was doing well on that front. The pain of losing his father was acute, but bearable. Matt suspected that was because he'd lost his father a long time ago, in spirit if not in body — since long before their argument, in fact. Matt's pop hadn't been the same since his mom had died. He'd tried every way he could think of to help his father over the years, even suggesting he see a grief counsellor to help him cope with the loss. But Hank had refused to admit there had been a problem—had said he was coping just fine. But he hadn't been coping just fine. He hadn't been coping at all.

Hank had been so heartsick that Matt had expected him to die years before. He knew people didn't actually die of a broken heart, at least that's what the medical profession would have you believe, but in the end it was his heart that had killed him, wasn't it? Expected or not, Matt still felt the loss—the grief an almost physical pain in his chest. The scariest thing was that Matt knew he was all alone in the world now. Hank had been the only family he'd had left. At least with James in his life, Matt wouldn't feel so lonely anymore. And he had Laney of course—his dear friend who had already served as his saviour once. She was a constant in Matt's life. Fiercely loyal and protective, she would always be there when Matt needed her.

All the time Matt had spent with James in the last few days made him remember the reasons they'd been friends to begin with. They had a lot of things in common and, even though they'd both grown up a lot over the last ten years and had gone on to lead somewhat different lives, that fact was still true. They liked the same football team—the St Louis Rams—and had the same taste in music—indie rock and a little country. They laughed at the same stupid jokes and enjoyed the same types of food. Neither was a morning person. Since Matt had made the decision to let go of the past, they had slipped back into their easy friendship as though it had never ended.

Matt was actually getting used to the idea of being in a relationship with James, although he still worried about James being in the closet. He hoped they wouldn't always have to hide the way they felt for one another, because Matt didn't think he'd be able to do that. He didn't want to live his life as though he had some dirty little secret, when he was in no way ashamed of who he was. Quite the opposite,

123

in fact. Matt was proud to be dating James and he couldn't be more proud of the men they'd both become. There were moments Matt had to pinch himself when he realised he had someone as great as James to call his partner — the man he'd dreamt about since they were in their teens.

James' mother had yet to talk to her son about what she'd overheard, and James was under the impression she needed more time to 'get her head around' what she'd learnt. Matt was convinced she'd had more than enough time, and he'd decided to give them a shove in the right direction. He was going to get them together after the funeral service so they could talk it out. The fact that he was burying his father proved that life was too damn short to hold a grudge against someone you loved.

James said he knew his mother didn't care he was gay, even though she'd seemed upset at first. Maria thought she was hurt because James hadn't told her himself, and Matt had to agree with her. It was probably the way she'd found out that was hardest thing for her to deal with. Feeling like she was the last person to know about what was going on in her own son's life would be a serious blow for any mother. She had a good relationship with James. They were close — or so she must have thought — and it must have hurt like hell that James had felt he couldn't talk to her about something so important to him.

Matt suspected Gladys was more upset because she hadn't suspected anything, like she should have had a sixth sense about it because he was her son. That had been one of the things his own father had said to him when Matt had told him he was gay. Then they'd had the argument and separation that had endured until his death. They'd said some mean things to one another during that argument and it had been the very last time Matt had spoken to Hank. He supposed he could understand how his pop would have felt like he didn't even know him. Maybe Gladys felt the same way.

Matt adjusted his tie in the mirror for the fifth time. It

hadn't moved an inch, but it was damn near choking the life out of him and there was no air in the house, either. Matt felt suffocated. James' face appeared in the mirror behind him and his hands came to rest on Matt's shoulders.

"The tie looks good, Matt." James offered him a reassuring smile.

Matt fiddled with the tie a little more, then nodded and dropped his hands. "Thanks for being here today."

James' eyebrows scrunched together. He turned Matt until they were face to face. "Where else would I be?"

Matt shrugged then dropped his gaze. "I don't know if I can do this," he whispered.

James shook his head then pressed a kiss against Matt's lips. "You can do this. You're stronger than you think, and I'll be right beside you every step of the way, okay?"

"I know." Matt felt as though a weight had been lifted since he'd started to put the past behind him and concentrate on the here and now. He believed that James was there for him and would continue to be. He didn't know when exactly over the last few days it had happened, but he trusted James implicitly now—cared about him. Well, it was more than that if he was being honest with himself. James was starting to mean everything to him and, although they hadn't discussed their feelings, he got the impression his were reciprocated. He certainly hoped so. James hadn't said or done anything to make him think otherwise.

"Laney is waiting downstairs for you," James said. "You ready to come down?"

Matt nodded. "I'll be right there. I just need another couple of minutes."

"No problem. I'll go and keep her company, leave you to it."

"Thanks," Matt said, meaning it. "For everything."

James patted his shoulder and left the bathroom, and Matt listened to his footsteps disappear down the stairs while he stared at his reflection in the mirror.

"You can do this," he said quietly to himself, repeating

James' words.

* * * *

More people attended the funeral service than Matt had expected. It seemed his father had made a lot of friends in his lifetime. Every seat in the small church had been filled with people paying their last respects. Matt bumbled his way through the prayers and hymns, Laney to his right and James giving him strength from the left. It was a lovely service, simple and understated. Just like Hank. Matt thought his father would have approved.

People lined up outside the church to tell Matt how sorry they were and to talk about their memories of Hank. Everyone had a story to tell. Matt tried to remember to invite everyone back to the house for refreshments, but he thought he might have missed a few people. Many said they couldn't make it and Matt was relieved. If everyone who had attended the funeral went back to his house, he wasn't sure they would all fit inside.

He needn't have worried. Only Hank's closest friends and associates came back to the house after they'd laid his father to rest in the graveyard across town from the church. That part had been even harder than the church ceremony for Matt. Seeing his father's casket lowered into the ground had caused a stabbing pain in his chest. Tears had prickled behind his eyes, but he'd kept them at bay, holding on to his grief and swallowing it down like a bitter pill until he could no longer taste it.

When he arrived home there were a few faces Matt didn't recognise, but mostly everyone who showed up, he remembered from his youth, even if he couldn't always put a name to the face.

Cups of tea and coffee made their way around the room along with sandwiches and trays full of butter cake and sweet pastries. James, Laney and Maria had taken care of all the food. Matt had insisted he pay them for the ingredients, but they'd shot him down flat. He'd have to think of some other way to repay them when he was actually able to think again. When his mind wasn't a jumble of sorrow and fear and names and faces that were all rolling into one.

As the day wore on, Matt started to get weary. He knew people had the best of intentions, but he was tired of making small talk. He just wanted the day to come to an end. He wanted to curl up on the sofa with James at his side and grieve for his father in peace. He'd have to wait a little while longer, though, it seemed.

"Mr Jacobs, you mind if we have a word with you?"

When Matt turned, he came face to face with Mrs McCormick and Mrs Peters – the town gossips and the bane of his father's existence from what Matt could remember. He suppressed a groan.

"Ladies," Matt greeted.

Mrs Peters reached out and put a hand on Matt's arm. "Hello, dear. We were so terribly sorry to hear of your father's death, weren't we, Betty?"

Betty McCormick shook her head. "Terrible news," she agreed.

"Thank you," Matt replied. He looked over the sisters' shoulders to see if he could spot James, but he was nowhere in the room.

"We wanted to have a chat with you about your father's responsibilities," Betty said.

May scowled at her sister. "Betty!" she chastised. "The poor man has just buried his father. He doesn't want you bothering him today."

"I wasn't bothering him." Betty rolled her eyes, fixed her gaze on Matt and ploughed on. "I was just curious if you'd be staying in town. Because you know your father was a very valuable member of the neighbourhood watch."

That came as a surprise. "He was?"

"Well yes, dear," May answered. "For several years. You should talk to your friend – that nice young man, James. He's been coming to meetings for a couple of years, too."

That was all new to Matt, but it certainly explained how James had been having conversations with his pop about him.

"I was planning on staying in town, yes," Matt told the sisters, "but I hadn't thought any further than that."

"Of course you haven't," May said. "You've had other things on your mind." She shot a dark look at her sister then patted Matt's arm.

"If you'd like to take your father's place in the watch, James can tell you the date of the next meeting."

Matt couldn't deal with this right now. He tugged at his tie and searched the room again. He didn't care about any damn neighbourhood watch and he certainly didn't want to think about taking his father's place, in anything. Right before he thought he would lose it, James appeared at his side and suddenly Matt could breathe again.

"Good afternoon, ladies. You don't mind if I steal Matt away from you, do you?"

"No, we—"

"Wonderful," James said, pulling Matt towards the kitchen. "Talk to you later."

They zigzagged through people as they made their way through the house, past the kitchen and into the back yard. It was only then that James let go of Matt's arm.

"Thanks for that," Matt said. "Thought I was going to lose it back there."

James shrugged. "Don't mention it. I saw you with the terrible twins and I suspected you'd need rescuing."

"You know, May isn't so bad, but her sister..." Matt shuddered.

"Yeah, tell me about it. She's as nervy as an army major and subtlety never was her strong point. Was she trying to rope you into something back there?"

"Neighbourhood watch."

James rolled his eyes. "I should have known. Sorry I didn't get to you sooner. I came as soon as I saw you."

Matt shrugged. "You never told me you were in the

neighbourhood watch programme with my dad."

"Didn't realise you didn't know," James replied.

"So, you spoke to my father a lot over the past couple of years?"

"Not a great deal, but yeah, we talked some. It was mainly neighbourhood watch business, but from time to time we spoke about you."

"And he didn't once mention our argument or the fact we hadn't spoken in so long?"

"No." James shrugged. "I don't know why. Maybe he was embarrassed. Didn't want anyone to know what a damn fool he'd been."

"Yeah, maybe," Matt agreed. "Although I was a damn fool, too."

"Was the argument you guys had really that bad?"

"Yeah," Matt said around a sigh. "It was bad. Pop said he never wanted to see me again."

"I don't believe he meant it."

"Yeah, I don't think he meant it, either—not really. At least, I hope he didn't, but it doesn't matter anymore, does it? It's too late to change anything. We both said some things to each other, things I know I wish I could take back. Knowing Pop, he'd want the same thing, but we were both too stubborn. Both waiting for the other to make the first move, you know?"

"I'm sure your father knew you didn't mean the things you said. Hank knew you loved him."

"I sure as hell hope so because I *did* love him." Matt offered a small smile. "Even though he could be a cantankerous old goat."

James placed his hand on Matt's shoulder. "He loved you too, Matt."

"I hope he's happy now, wherever he is. I hope he's with my mom."

"I hope so too." James leant forward and pressed a soft kiss against Matt's lips. It was barely a whisper of flesh against flesh, but it made Matt instantly more relaxed. He rested his hands on James' shoulders and pressed his lips against James.

"Thank you," he whispered.

A loud gasp at the door had James pulling back and when Matt looked over his shoulder the look of horror on Betty McCormick's face made him shiver.

"I..." All of the colour drained out of James' cheeks and he looked as though he might throw up. Matt felt for him, he really did, but it was out of his hands. There could be no denying what they were doing — not that Matt would have — but the panic visible on James' face said that he might have, given half the chance. It was by no means a passionate kiss, but it was a kiss nonetheless. Men didn't go around kissing their platonic friends on the lips — or anywhere else for that matter. And Betty McCormick wasn't stupid.

Her expression hardened. "Just what is going on here?"

Matt opened his mouth to tell her it was none of her goddamn business when James beat him to the punch. "I was comforting Matt. In case you'd forgotten, he just buried his father. Is that okay with you, or do I need your permission before I kiss my boyfriend in the future?"

James' words sent a thrill of excitement through Matt's body. He was under no illusions. He knew that given the choice James would never have come out in that way, if at all — especially to the likes of Betty McCormick — but he'd just publicly declared them an item regardless. He might have only told one person, but it was a start.

"Are you telling me you're gay?" she spluttered, staring at James with a glare that would have floored a lesser man. Okay, maybe she wasn't as bright as Matt had first thought.

"Yes, he is." Gladys stood in the doorway behind Betty. Matt hadn't even noticed her there until she spoke. She winked at Matt then walked to James' side and took hold of his arm, showing Betty and anyone else that might have anything to say about it that James was still her son and she loved him. "Do you have a problem with that?"

Betty's mouth fell open and she stared at Gladys, her

face growing redder with every passing second. Matt had never seen her at a loss for words before. It made a pleasant change.

"I think you should go inside and find your sister," Gladys said. "She was looking under the weather when I just saw her. I think it would be best if you took her home."

Betty didn't reply, just turned on her heel and, with a last frosty gaze at each of them, she slipped back inside the house.

* * * *

"Uncle James!" Hope came barrelling into the diner and collided into James' leg. He scooped her up, gave her a quick hug then tickled her side, which had her in fits of giggles and squirming helplessly in his arms. "No, please! Let me down!"

James chuckled and finally relented, but instead of putting her back down on her feet, he set her on one of the stools at the counter.

"Where's Matt?" she asked as soon as she stopped giggling.

"Matt is at home, honey. I'll tell him you were asking about him, okay?"

Hope nodded. "Okay."

"What's up, sis?" James asked when he noticed the frown on his sister's face.

"Just what the hell do you think you're playing at?"

James let out a long sigh. "What did I do now?"

"It's been two weeks since you called. Are you trying to tell me something?" He could always count on his sister to be melodramatic.

"I've been busy," James said over his shoulder while he made them a cup of coffee. "And I've been spending a lot of time over at Matt's place."

"I'm not complaining about the time you spend with Matt. I'm happy for you both, you know that, but a five-minute phone call wouldn't go amiss."

James tried out the puppy-dog eyes that Matt sometimes used on him, but he didn't think it worked so well with his bright-blue eyes. When Matt gave him the look with his big chocolate-brown eyes, it made James want to fall at his feet and promise him the world. Besides, Maria had practice with the puppy-dog eyes—Hope pulled them every time she was trying to get her own way. He gave up.

"Will sorry cut it?" he finally asked.

"It's a start." Maria grinned wickedly. "But a free cup of coffee might make me feel even more charitable."

James rolled his eyes. "Since when did you have to pay for coffee here? And, besides, the phone works both ways, you know. You could try calling me once in a while. And one of the reasons I didn't call is because you usually come in during the week. Has someone been keeping *you* busy, huh?"

James chuckled when a blush spread across Maria's cheeks. She averted her gaze.

"Ah and now it all makes perfect sense. Have you been spending more time with a certain dentist?"

"I might have been."

Hope's head had been swivelling back and forth, listening to their conversation.

"Is he talking about John, Mommy? John's a dentist."

James laughed and gave his sister a knowing grin. They couldn't discuss anything in Hope's presence anymore without her wanting to know what the conversation was about. Maria pinched one of Hope's cheeks.

"Yes, he is. Tell Uncle James what John bought you."

Hope spun around on her stool so fast she nearly fell off. Maria's hand shot out and grabbed her just in time. Hope didn't even blink. Her face became animated and full of the type of excitement only a five-year-old could possess. "He bought me a Barbie princess and a dog!"

"Wow! That's incredible, poppet." James raised a curious eyebrow at his sister. "Not a real one, I trust."

132

Maria snorted. "No, James, get with the programme. A dog for Barbie."

"Gotcha. Isn't it a little soon for him to be buying gifts?"

"They weren't for me," Maria said defensively. "Not that I'd complain, but if he wants to buy Hope a gift I'm not going to stop him."

James shook his head. It sounded to him like John was trying to buy his way into Maria's affections and was using Hope to do it. But maybe James was just being cynical. John had seemed like a nice enough guy. Maybe he was just generous. James hoped that was the case because he could tell Maria liked him, and he could easily see her growing to love him.

He didn't think it was a good idea for John to be seeing Hope so much yet, either. Shouldn't his sister have waited until they'd been together for a while longer before she introduced him to Hope? What if they split up and Hope was already attached to him? That could really hurt her and James didn't want to see that happen to his niece. But Hope was Maria's daughter, he didn't have much of a say in how she was raised. She would only tell him to butt out if he asked her about it.

Maria looked around the diner and raised a curious eyebrow. "It's quiet in here, isn't it? What the hell happened? You been poisoning people with your butter cake?"

James shrugged. "Just a quiet day, is all. It'll pick up." The truth was the diner had been quiet for a few days— ever since the funeral, in fact. James didn't want to believe that Betty McCormick had had anything to do with his sudden lack of customers, but quite frankly he couldn't think of any other reason why people would be keeping away. Betty loved to gossip and that gossip was sometimes of a malicious nature. James wouldn't be surprised if most of the town knew about his orientation by now. He'd seen neither hide nor hair of her or her sister since the funeral, and he'd only had a handful of customers come in all day. If business stayed this quiet, he wouldn't be able to afford to stay open. He could cope with the drop in earnings for a little while, sure, but not long-term.

"Has Mom called?"

James placed a cup of coffee on the counter in front of his sister and a soda for Hope. He took a sip of his own coffee before replying. "Nope."

Even though his mom had stood by his side against Betty at the funeral, they hadn't spoken since. James knew they needed to talk through their problems, but his mother's actions at the funeral and her subsequent absence told James she wasn't ready to forgive him for not telling her yet.

"And it didn't cross your mind to call her?"

"Not you, too. Please, sis, I get enough nagging about this from Matt."

"I'm glad to hear it. I knew there was a reason I liked that man. So are you going to listen to either of us for a change?"

"If Mom wants to talk to me, she'll call."

"You stubborn... Haven't you learned anything from Matt's situation? What if something happens to Mom before the two of you make up? How would you be able to live with yourself?"

James' stomach lurched at the thought. "She's not ill, is she?"

"Why don't you ask her?" Maria shrugged.

Brat. "Maria!"

"No, she's not ill, but she's not a young woman anymore either. She won't be around forever."

"I know that."

"Then swallow your damn pride and give her a call or you might live to regret it."

What James didn't want to tell his sister was that he was afraid to call their mom. He was afraid to see her. He didn't want to see the disappointment in her eyes when she looked at him—he couldn't stomach that. But he knew Maria was right. He had to make the first move. He had to be the one to apologise first and to thank her for standing by his side at the funeral.

The trouble was James knew how much his mother disliked Betty McCormick, even though he didn't know the reason why. They'd been enemies for many years, although his mother wouldn't tell him what they'd fought over. A part of him was worried that she'd just stuck up for him because it would get under Betty's skin. They were always doing things they knew would annoy the other. He didn't want to believe his mother could be that shallow, but why hadn't she called him since the funeral?

"I'll call her today, okay? And if she doesn't answer the damn phone, I'll go to see her after work."

Maria nodded. "Now you're talking like the brother I know and love."

James grinned wickedly at his sister and placed a menu in front of Hope. When Maria groaned, he chuckled and pointed to the triple chocolate sundae. "Order anything you want, honey."

* * * *

Matt looked at the clock on the kitchen wall as he lowered the heat on the pasta, a small smile playing on his lips. He and James had been spending more and more time together over the week since his father's funeral. James had come to his house every evening after he finished his shift in the diner. They had eaten together, watched television, talked. They were beginning to settle into a routine that seemed to suit them both. James had slept over nearly every night, too, and bedtime had fast become Matt's favourite time of day. He tried to keep himself busy during the long days he was alone in the house and always looked forward to James' arrival, which eased his loneliness and boredom.

Although Matt had needed to take some time for himself, he knew he couldn't sit around the house forever. He had to go back to Iowa soon. His house was sitting empty and if he was serious about staying in Missouri and making a life for himself with James then he had to get back there to pack up his belongings and ship them home. He'd have to meet with a Realtor to put his house on the market or look at renting it out. And when he got back to Missouri, he had to start looking for a job. His pop had left him some money, but Matt would burn through it quickly if he didn't have a wage coming in. He couldn't afford to let that happen.

He was stirring in the pasta sauce when he heard the front door open and James' voice sound down the hall.

"Matt, I'm home!"

Those three little words made butterflies dance in Matt's stomach. Did James realise the effect he had on him? He was able to turn Matt on just by walking in a room, but when he said something like that — talked about home or family without even realising what he was saying — it made Matt's heart swell. James poked his head around the door and a wide grin spread across his face.

"Hey." He crossed the room and planted a kiss on Matt's lips. "You cooked."

"Pasta okay for you?"

"Perfect, but I thought we were going out to eat."

"Apparently the Italian gets busy. We needed to reserve a table, so I booked one for next weekend if that's okay for you. If not, I can ring and cancel."

James shrugged. "Next weekend's good." He slid his arms around Matt's waist until they came to rest on his stomach. Matt thought James was just giving him a hug, but then he inched one hand up his chest, the fingertips gliding over his sensitive nipples while he moved his other hand lower, pressing it against the bulge in his pants. Matt gasped and automatically bucked into James' hand.

Pressing against him from behind, James let out a low moan. "God, what a great way to start the evening." He continued rubbing and stroking with his hands while he gently rocked against Matt from behind, his erection hard and insistent against Matt's ass. When James began to nuzzle the back of his neck, it made gooseflesh rise on Matt's arms and his head fell back and to the side instinctually, giving James better access. He gave up all pretence of stirring the pasta and just enjoyed James' hands on him.

"Don't you want to eat?"

He felt rather than saw James' smile against his neck. "That's what microwaves are for. Besides I'd rather eat you."

Matt chuckled and turned in James' arms. "Did I ever tell you I like the way you think?"

"You might have mentioned it. But you could always tell me again."

"I like..." Matt didn't get any further into the sentence before James tilted his head to the side and captured Matt's mouth, pushing his tongue inside as though it belonged there. Matt didn't know how it happened, but the next thing he knew he was lying on the kitchen floor, James on top of him, grinding their hips together while they shared a hard, demanding kiss.

James pulled back to catch a breath and the heated look in his eyes made Matt ache with need. James held his gaze while he unbuttoned Matt's pants and pulled them and his briefs roughly down his hips. He didn't waste any time teasing. He went straight for the prize and took Matt's cock in his mouth, sucking it right down to the base.

"Oh fuck," Matt groaned, his hips jerking upwards to meet James' mouth as if of their own accord. James sucked him hard, just the way he liked it, but when Matt's moans and whimpers got louder and more desperate, filling the quiet air around them, he backed off and laved the head of Matt's cock with his tongue, before dipping it inside the slit.

"Do they give out prizes for that?" Matt asked breathlessly and James had to pull back or choke when he laughed.

"Why, would I get one?"

"Hell yeah, first goddamn place. Jesus, but you can suck cock. Drives me damn near insane."

James' only response was a wicked grin before his warm,

wet tongue found the sensitive spot below Matt's balls and the need in Matt rose to epic proportions. He thought the desire he felt for James was unparalleled until he looked down into James' eyes and saw the lust shining back at him and realised he wasn't alone in his feelings. Not even close.

"Jesus, James... Suck me, please." Matt couldn't stand it much longer. But James wasn't even close to being finished with him.

"This what you want?" James asked before he took Matt to the back of his throat and swallowed. Matt's brain short-circuited and he couldn't reply. He was barely hanging on to his sanity.

James' mouth was relentless as he slid up and down his cock. Matt hissed and reached down to tangle his fingers in James' hair, but he tried not to pull too hard on it and resisted bucking his hips up into the tight, wet heat of James' mouth. Up and down James slid on his cock, increasing the pressure with every pass while he kneaded Matt's heavy sac and stroked his perineum, inching his fingers towards his entrance. When James added a scrape of teeth on every upstroke and swirled his tongue around the head, the tip of his finger pressing just inside his ass, it was all over for Matt.

"Oh fuck, I can't last anymore, gonna come," Matt ground out. "Ungh!" His grip in James' hair tightened and he came hard, emptying the contents of his balls into James' mouth. James swallowed him down and licked the head of his cock to capture the last few drops while Matt still trembled from the aftershocks. When he looked down he realised James was staring at him, his expression full of wonder.

"I'll never get tired of watching you like that," James whispered.

Matt reached for James and pulled him up for a kiss, tasting himself in his lover's mouth. He reached a hand between them and grabbed hold of James through his jeans. James gasped and bucked into the touch. When he pulled back from the kiss, Matt chuckled.

"Do you realise your crotch is vibrating?"

"Huh?" The dazed expression on James' face only lasted for a moment before he snapped into action and pulled the cell phone out of his pocket and answered the call.

"Hello?" James' happy expression faded while he listened to the caller. "Is she...?"

James closed his eyes and nodded his head. "I'll be right there," he said before ending the call.

All of the colour had drained out of James' face. Matt reached for his hand and held it in his own. "What's wrong?"

"That was Maria," James replied. "She was calling from the hospital. It's Mom. She's ill. They think it's her heart..."

Matt squeezed James' hand for reassurance even as his own stomach jolted and the vision of his pop lying cold in the hospital bed sprang to mind.

"She's going to be okay," he said quickly, but he wasn't sure who he was trying to convince.

139

Chapter Eight

James strode through the hospital corridor on autopilot. The noises that were going on around him hardly registered as he focused single-mindedly on finding his sister. Just as he pushed through another set of swinging doors, Matt grabbed hold of his arm.

"You sure you don't want me to wait in the car? I don't know that I should be here."

James frowned. He couldn't believe he'd been such an ass. He'd been so worried about getting to see his mom that he hadn't stopped to think about how difficult this would be for Matt. The last time he'd been to this hospital he'd been saying goodbye to his pop.

"Christ, I'm sorry. Of course you should wait in the car. I didn't even think, Matt. Must be so hard for you to be here. Why didn't you say anything? I appreciate you wanting to be here for me, but, Jesus, you should have said no."

Matt shook his head. "It is hard being back here, but I meant what I said. I'm here for you. But I wasn't talking about that. I just meant that... Well, your family will be here and I..."

James frowned then reached out and cupped Matt's jaw. "You are my family now, too."

Matt nodded. "Then I'm staying here."

"James."

James' head swivelled when he heard his sister's voice.

"Maria, what's going on?"

Maria took a deep breath. "She's okay. Just had a bit of a scare. The doctor said she had a minor heart attack so they're keeping her in for a few days for observation. She's

140

currently having thrombolysis."

James didn't like the sound of that one little bit. "What's that?"

"It's treatment that will dissolve the blood clot and restore the flow of blood to her heart. Apparently she had difficulty breathing, but the doctor said it was just a small amount of fluid on her lung so they've drained it and she's using an oxygen mask to help her breathe. It sounds scary, I know, but the doctor said there's no reason she shouldn't make a full recovery from this."

James finally allowed himself to take a breath. "She could have died," he whispered.

Maria nodded and grabbed hold of James' hand. "But she didn't and she's not going to, not yet. She's a fighter. She just needs to slow down. She can't keep going at the pace she has been, she works too damn hard. The doctor just told her the same thing and I think she's finally going to listen. This scared her, James."

"Damn well scared us all." James sighed. He gave a cursory glance down the corridor behind his sister. "Where's Hope?"

"Her father came to pick her up a while ago, but I think he's going to drop her off at his parents' place. He said he was busy."

James rolled his eyes. "What, he can't look after her for one night?"

Maria shrugged. "Guess not. Hope loves her grams and grandpa, though, so as long as she's happy…"

"How are you holding up, Maria?" Matt asked.

"Oh, you know me—balls of steel," she joked.

Just as she intended, Matt chuckled, but James had neither the energy nor the inclination to curve his mouth up into a smile. "Does she… Does she want to see me?" he asked in a small voice that was barely audible over the din of the busy hospital.

"Of course she does, James—she loves you." Maria shook her head. "If she wasn't ill I swear I'd knock your goddamn heads together. Might do it anyway."

"I've been promising the same thing," Matt said.

"Lucy and Will are on their way here."

James nodded. "Do you think it will be all right if I go in and see her now?" he asked.

Maria placed a comforting hand on James' shoulder. "Of course. She's waiting for you."

After Maria had given James directions to their mother's ward, he gave her a hug and left her with Matt. Butterflies danced in his stomach as he made his way along the corridor. He wasn't even sure why he was so nervous. It was partly because he hadn't spoken to his mother since before the funeral. Even though she'd stood up for him there against Betty McCormick, he was still afraid he would see disappointment in her eyes when she looked at him. But mostly it was because of what had happened to her. It brought home how very fragile life could be, how precious. He didn't want to have to think about his mother's mortality. But having already lost his pop and Matt having lost both his parents, he knew the cold, hard reality. He stopped short just inside the door to her ward and sucked in a sharp breath when he caught his first glimpse of her.

Gladys was sitting up in bed, but she had the covers pulled up to her chest and she was still wearing the oxygen mask. She looked pale and more frail than James had ever thought possible. He hated seeing her like that. His mother had never been fragile—even when she was recovering from losing her husband, she had seemed stronger than she did now. James' stomach roiled. He took a deep breath and walked farther into the room. Gladys' head turned in his direction and a wide smile broke out across her delicate face behind the mask. The expression made her look a little better, but not much.

"James," she croaked. "I'm so glad you're here."

When James reached the bed his mother held out her hand for him to take. James grabbed it and held it in his own. "Hey, Mom. How are you feeling?"

"I've been better," she replied.

James nodded and felt a lump form in his throat. "Mom, I'm so sorry for everything."

Gladys shook her head. "You have nothing to apologise for. I was just...surprised. I'm sorry. I should have handled it better."

"No, I should have told you about me a long time ago."

His mom smiled through her mask. "Maybe, yes. I think that upset me most, that you felt you couldn't talk to me about it. What did you think I was going to say?"

"I don't know," James replied. It was the truth. He wasn't sure why he'd never told his mother. It could have been the same reason he'd never come out. Fear of rejection, maybe? James didn't want to be treated like a pariah. He didn't want people he'd grown up with to suddenly cross the street when they saw him. He didn't think he could handle people talking about him behind his or his family's backs. And what of his family, would they suffer because of James? Would Hope get teased in school if some of the other children heard their parents talk about it?

But James supposed the main reason he hadn't said anything was because he simply didn't like discussing his sexuality. He didn't want to talk to people about what he did in bed and with whom. And even though he was now seeing Matt and was happier than he could ever remember being, he still didn't want all that other stuff that came with it. He had no idea how he'd cope with any of it and hoped he didn't have to find out. Matt was an open book. He liked living his life that way. He would rather live an honest life than one where he had to hide. That was great in theory, but James wasn't sure the reality of it was something he was capable of. And then where would that leave things between them? Could Matt be truly happy with someone who lived their life in the shadows?

"It doesn't matter," Gladys said. "I'd really like if we could put it behind us and start over."

James let out a sigh of relief. "I'd like that too, Mom. More than I can say." James was quiet for a moment while he stroked his mom's hand then he looked up and met her eye. "This is my fault, isn't it? This happened because of me. The stress and the…"

"No!" Gladys said fiercely. She lowered her breathing mask and stared at him defiantly. "This had nothing to do with you, so don't you go blaming yourself. I'm in here because I was stupid. Because I was doing too much, should have slowed down and should have listened to people when they told me my lifestyle wasn't the healthiest. There are lots of reasons I'm in here, and none of them have anything to do with you or the fact you're gay. You understand?"

James swallowed down the lump in his throat. "Okay."

"So…" Gladys lowered her gaze and a faint blush spread across her cheeks. The sudden colour made her look healthier. "Are you seeing anyone right now?"

James nodded. He couldn't stop the smile that spread across his face when he thought about Matt. He always had the capacity to make James smile, usually without trying. He just had to walk in a room and James' heart lifted. "Yeah, Mom, I'm seeing Matt."

Gladys raised her eyebrows in surprise, but then she, too, smiled. "Well, I'm glad. Such a lovely boy. And since his father's gone, he's all alone in the world."

James shook his head. "Not anymore, he isn't."

Gladys slipped the mask back over her mouth and James continued to stroke the back of her hand, watching as her eyes drifted shut. When she fell asleep, a small smile still covered her lips. He sat with her for a while, watching her relaxed face until his baby sister came and tapped him on the shoulder and pulled him up for a hug that was barely possible with her enormous baby bump jutting out between them.

* * * *

"Hey," Matt greeted brightly as he strode through the

144

diner. James was leaning against the counter, his arms folded and a faraway expression on his face. "How's your day been?"

Matt leaned over to kiss him on the cheek, but James pushed him away and cast a panicked look around the empty diner as though Matt had just committed an offence that could get them both stoned.

Matt frowned. The James he got at home and the James he was in public were like two different people. He didn't recognise this James, and he was sorry to admit he didn't like him very much, either. For a moment he was transported back to his time with Tom when he was made to feel like he was nothing more than a dirty secret that had to be hidden out of sight.

"What the hell? There's no one here and I hardly got down on my knees and stuck your cock in my mouth. It was a kiss on the cheek, for Chrissake."

"I'm sorry," James sighed. "But, Jesus, can't you cut me some slack? You might have been out since you were eighteen, but this is still new for me."

"I realise that, but sometimes… Well, you act like you're ashamed of me, ashamed of us."

"I'm not ashamed of you. I just…" He shook his head. "This is not easy for me."

Matt tried not to let James' words upset him because, despite his actions, he knew James cared for him, but some things were easier said than done. For Matt, being with James was as easy as breathing and it stung that James didn't feel the same way.

Will he ever?

The thought stole Matt's breath and he quickly changed the subject to a topic that didn't have the capacity to do his heart even more damage.

"Where is everyone, anyway?" His gaze slid around the empty diner. He'd never seen the place so quiet.

"Don't know," James mumbled. "You want a cup of coffee?"

Matt took a seat on one of the high stools and leaned his arms on the counter. "Please. How is your mom doing today?" James had left his house early that morning so he could call by the hospital before he started his shift.

"Good. She seems to be getting better every day. The doctor said, if her progress continues, she can go home in a few days."

"I bet she can't wait to get out of there."

James shook his head. "I'm not so sure. She gets lonely at home and I think she's enjoying all the attention she's getting in there. I've yet to see her on her own. Her colleagues are constantly stopping by her bedside for a chat."

"Is she going to go back to work?"

"I don't know," James sighed. "She shouldn't. The doctor told her to take it easy, but she's so stubborn. It really is time she thought about retiring. I haven't spoken to her about it because I don't want to nag while she's lying in a hospital bed recovering from a heart attack, you know? But I'm afraid if I don't say anything, if none of us do…" James shrugged. "She needs to know how we all feel about this, about how much her decision affects us, too."

"Your mother might be stubborn, but she's not stupid. If the doctor told her to take it easy then I'm sure she'll listen to him, especially after what just happened to her."

"I hope you're right."

James placed two cups of steaming hot coffee on the counter and took the stool next to Matt's.

"Is your sister still in town?"

James took a sip of coffee before he spoke. "Yeah, Lucy's staying with Maria until the end of the week, and then Will is going to come back to take her home."

"He couldn't stay any longer himself?"

"No, he got time off work, but they thought it best if one of them was at home with Justin. They left him with Will's mom when they came up, but she's about the same age as my mom, and Justin…well, he's four. He can be a handful."

Matt chuckled. "I can imagine. So you all set for the meal

at the Italian place tonight?"

"Wouldn't miss it," James said, but he was staring into his coffee cup when he spoke and didn't look up to meet Matt's gaze. Matt couldn't be sure, but he thought he saw James' shoulders stiffen and his eyebrows pull together before his expression cleared, giving nothing else away.

* * * *

James and Matt followed the waiter to their table at the back of the restaurant. It was a nice place. Most of the walls were exposed brick and the lighting was low, atmospheric. The tables were covered in white linen and the silverware looked as though it really was made of silver. James looked down at his pale-blue shirt tucked into beige pants and wished he'd put on something more formal or at least worn a tie. Better yet, he wished they hadn't come. The restaurant was very nearly full and all eyes seemed to follow them to their table, or at least that's what it felt like.

James wished he could be more like Matt. He was walking through the room with a confidence that just radiated from him. His shoulders were squared and he was standing tall. Matt didn't seem to notice that people were watching them, and if he did, he didn't act like he cared. They thanked the waiter and took their seats. Matt was smiling and, even though James felt nervous and on edge, he couldn't help the way that smile affected him. It brightened everything just like a ray of sunshine on a stormy day.

"Nice place," Matt commented, picking up the wine menu and scanning its contents.

"Yeah, yeah it is."

"Any idea what you'd like to drink?"

The woman at the next table caught James' eye and when she glanced at Matt then leaned across the table to whisper something to her friend, he quickly looked away, feeling his cheeks fill with heat. "Uh, I'll just have a beer."

"Oh." Matt put the wine menu down and shrugged.

"Okay."

James lowered his gaze and chewed on a hangnail. This was harder than he'd anticipated. Why the hell had he agreed to come? He could feel his heart racing in his chest, feel his palms getting sweaty. He hated that everyone was watching them. What the hell did they find so interesting? It was only two friends having dinner together. Only they weren't *just* friends anymore, were they? And it felt like everyone knew that and was judging him. Maybe Matt wouldn't mind if they left, got takeout and stayed at home. No. He had to calm down, damn it. It was only dinner. They'd eat and then they could get the hell out of there.

"Is everything okay?" Matt asked.

"Yeah. Why wouldn't it be?" James' reply came out snappier than he'd intended and Matt flinched.

"You don't seem like yourself," he said quietly.

When the waiter reappeared at their table they ordered drinks—a bottle of beer for James and a large glass of chianti for Matt. As soon as he'd left, James picked up his menu and scanned its contents—anything to avoid Matt's eye. He knew he was acting like an idiot, but he didn't know how to change. He didn't feel comfortable in his own skin, didn't know if he ever would.

There was a lot to choose from on the menu and it all looked good. James usually ordered ravioli when he ate in Italian restaurants, but the gnocchi sounded too good to pass up on. He was still deciding when a familiar voice pulled him from his thoughts.

"James, that you?" When he looked up, Mr Keller, the old art teacher, was standing at their table, his floppy blond hair swishing as his head swivelled back and forth between him and Matt. James groaned inwardly. He had nothing against Mr Keller, but he was pretty...well, *camp*, and people were already staring.

James cursed himself for caring so much what people thought and reached out to shake his hand. "Mr Keller, good to see you. You remember Matt? Matt Jacobs?"

Mr Keller's smile got even bigger. He reached out and shook Matt's hand. "Yes—yes, of course I do. It's good to see you again, Matt. Are you living here in Providence again or are you just visiting?"

"I've actually moved home now, sir."

Mr Keller rolled his eyes. "We're not in high school anymore. Please, call me Chris. I'd like to introduce you to my partner, Rory. I don't know if you all remember each other."

James turned and nearly choked on his surprise. He'd known Mr Keller had a partner in town, but he hadn't known who he was seeing. Rory Myers was a few years older than Matt and James. He'd been on the football team in school. He'd been James' one and only hookup from Providence after having bumped into him in a bar in St Louis. It had been a couple of years ago, and had only ever happened the once, but James couldn't contain his embarrassment. He could feel the heat rising in his cheeks. He squirmed in his seat, but shook Rory's hand and forced out a smile.

"Good to see you again, Rory."

Rory nodded and shook his and Matt's hands in turn. "You too."

"Look, we haven't even ordered yet," Matt said. "Would you care to join us?"

James nearly choked on his beer.

"Thank you for the offer," Mr Keller replied. "But we wouldn't want to impose and this is sort of a special night for us—our anniversary. First year together. Hope you understand."

Relief rushed through James and he shook his head. "No need to explain, of course we understand, and congratulations."

"Congratulations," Matt echoed. "That's wonderful news."

"We think so."

James felt ashamed at how relieved he was when the waiter showed Mr Keller and Rory to their own table.

How did people do this? Live out and proud and not let people's opinions affect them? More to the point, what was wrong with him that he couldn't? He was happy with Matt, happier than he could remember being, so why was it so difficult to actually be seen out in public with him? Why did he feel like there was a weight pressing down on his chest making it difficult for him to breathe?

"James?" Matt reached across the table and grabbed James' hand and before he could stop himself, James snatched his hand away. When he looked up, the hurt in Matt's eyes stole his breath. He hated himself for putting that look on Matt's face, hated that he was capable of it. He wanted to reach out to Matt and to reassure him that it would all be all right, but he didn't want to lie.

"I..." He didn't know what he was trying to say, but whatever it was, the words wouldn't come out of his mouth.

Matt's features hardened then, and he stared at James for a long moment with something that looked like resolve. He looked tired all of a sudden—bone-weary.

"I can't do this," Matt said, his voice raw with emotion. "I can't do this again."

James wanted to ask Matt what he meant by that, but it was too late for questions. He could see that, could feel it all the way down to his toes. And the nervous expectation became like a lead weight in his stomach when Matt lifted his hand and summoned the waiter.

Oh God. This is it. This is really it, isn't it? This is the part you were dreading and expecting all at the same time. This is the part where he gets up, walks away and doesn't look back and it's all your fucking fault. Dumbass. Say something, say anything. Get down on your knees and beg if you have to. Anything to get him to change his mind, to make him stay. Don't let him leave you.

James remained quiet while Matt spoke to the waiter and apologised for having to leave before dinner. He was quiet while Matt paid for the drinks and gave an extra large tip for the trouble. He was quiet while Matt got up from the table and told him goodnight. A part of him delighted in the word goodnight because it wasn't goodbye, but as Matt brushed past him, the look in his eyes told James the words could very well be interchangeable. A sorrow unlike any he'd known took hold of him and refused to let him out of its grasp. A very small part of him was aware he still had time. It wasn't too late yet. He could make things right. He could catch up with Matt and make him listen. He could beg him to understand and to give him more time. Maybe with more time…

But the lead weight in his stomach was like an anchor holding him in place, keeping him rooted firmly to the seat. The minutes ticked on, then it *was* too late to do anything but hate himself for being afraid, for being a coward and for letting Matt down…again.

Chapter Nine

"You look like shit."

James shrugged his shoulders and avoided his sister's penetrating gaze. He'd tried not to look in a mirror for the past few days, but if he looked even half as bad as he felt, he figured his sister had it spot on.

"Haven't been sleeping much," he confessed.

Maria ran her finger around the rim of her glass. "You surprised about that? How long has it been since he left? A couple of weeks?"

Sixteen days. "About that," James answered.

It had been sixteen days since Matt had walked out of his life. They hadn't seen each other since the fateful night at the restaurant and hadn't spoken either. James had lost count of the times he'd decided to go to Matt's house to apologise and to beg for his forgiveness. He would have given anything just to see Matt's beautiful face again or to feel the warmth of his body as he held him close, but each time he'd changed his mind at the last minute. Because it wouldn't have been fair to Matt. It would have been a lie. Not a lie that he was sorry—he was, more than he could vocalise. But he couldn't promise he wouldn't do it again and Matt deserved better than that.

It was no excuse but James had spent his entire life hiding that part of himself from the world and he was damn good at it. It wasn't something he could change overnight, it didn't matter how much he wished otherwise. It was ingrained into him, practically embedded in his DNA. He didn't want to be *that* man. But he didn't know how to be anything else.

Then one afternoon about a week ago, when he'd got back

from the diner, there had been a message on his answering machine. His heart had leapt when he'd first heard Matt's voice, but as his words had begun to sink in, James had slid down the wall until he was seated on the floor, his head planted between his legs. The deep breaths he'd sucked in had only barely stopped the feeling of sickness that was bubbling up in his chest.

"Hey. I'm on my way back to Iowa today. I just wanted to say that… I'm sorry it didn't work out between us." A sigh. *"Take care of yourself, James."*

So that was it. It really was over. James had listened to the message a second time and then a third. But it didn't matter how many times he played it, the outcome was always the same. Matt was telling him goodbye and for real this time.

It had been sixteen days that had stretched out into one long fucking nightmare of getting up and going through the motions and missing Matt so goddamn much he didn't know how he could live through it. And with each day that had passed, James had felt worse than the one before.

"Why haven't you called him?"

James wanted to shout and rage and scream. *Yeah, why the fuck haven't you called him, dumbass?* Instead he shook his head. "There's no point. I ruined everything. He forgave me for hurting him once before and he gave me a second chance, but I blew it. He won't be able to forgive me again."

"You sure about that?" Maria asked. "You know, you could always beg. Might work."

James knew his sister wasn't making light of the situation, she was just trying to make him smile again, but he didn't feel capable of holding the expression on his face, let alone the sentiment behind the smile. "He already gave me too many chances. No, he's better off without me."

"That's a line of crap, James. He loves you and you love him, so how can either of you be better off apart?"

He and Matt had never actually said the words out loud to each other, but James hadn't needed to hear them—he'd felt them. Every damn day they were together in every little thing Matt did. It was there, as clear and as bold as a neon flashing sign. Matt wore his heart on his sleeve and he displayed his feelings proudly. James wished more than anything he'd been able to do the same. Why couldn't he? What the hell was wrong with him that he hadn't been able to give Matt the one thing that he'd needed more than anything else? If his relationship with Matt had been the best thing that had ever happened to him, and he'd thrown it away because he was too scared of what a few people around town thought of him? Then he didn't deserve Matt.

"He deserves someone better than me," he said, voicing his innermost thoughts.

"Maybe he just deserves a better you, you thought about that?"

James stared at his sister long and hard. He had thought about that. Matter of fact, he'd thought about nothing else. He just wished he knew how to better himself so that he could be everything that Matt needed him to be. But that would assume Matt would actually care about taking him back. And that was a lot to ask. Too much? James was about to answer his sister when the bell above the door chimed. James glanced across the room, surprised to see Jane and Brittany — the two girls who worked at the mall — stroll in and take their usual seats near the window. James hadn't seen them since before Hank's funeral. He hadn't expected to see them again either.

He'd assumed they'd heard about his sexuality from Betty McCormick and didn't approve — boycotting the diner in protest. But here they were, smiling shyly and flicking their hair in their usual flirty manner. *The hell?* James' curiosity got the better of him. He picked up a couple of menus and carried them across the room.

"Hello, ladies, good to see you again." James handed each of them a menu, but they shook their heads and handed them back.

"That's okay, thanks," Jane said. "We know what we want. We'll take a couple of cups of coffee and two slices of

154

your peach and pecan pie."

"Sure thing. It's been a few weeks since I last saw you. You been keeping busy?" James doubted they'd admit the reason they hadn't been in, but it was worth a shot.

Brittany turned a fierce shade of red. "Yeah, uh, sorry we haven't been in for a while," she said quietly. "But we were taking advantage of the special offer at the new diner down the road."

James cocked his head to the side in confusion. "New diner?"

Jane nodded. "Haven't you heard about it? It's just around the corner from here. They opened a few weeks ago and they had a special discount offer during their first few weeks. Everything was half price. But the offer has ended now and, to tell you the truth, the food there isn't half as good as it is here. All our friends said the same thing. They're all going to come back here, too."

James couldn't believe what he was hearing. That was the reason it had been so quiet? Competition? Not because of his sexuality? He shook his head incredulously.

"I thought maybe you were staying away because you found out about my boyfriend," he blurted. Immediately he felt his face heat with embarrassment. He couldn't quite believe the words had left his mouth, but once they were out he couldn't take them back and he really didn't want to. They were the truth. Matt *had* been his boyfriend, his partner, the love of his life. It was just a shame he hadn't been able to admit that out loud while they were together. In public, not just when they were alone.

"Huh? Your *boyfriend*? You're gay?" Brittany asked.

James nodded a reply and squared his shoulders, feeling braver with every passing second. "Yeah...yeah, I am." He eyed the two women defiantly, daring them to say something out of turn.

Jane shook her head. James had expected shock, disdain even, but she was grinning broadly. "Well, damn. It's always the good-looking guys. Typical."

James snapped out of his trance while Brittany nodded her agreement.

"Right, uh, I guess I'll get your order," he mumbled, half to himself.

They were discussing the new shoe sale at the mall before he got back to his sister's side. Maria raised an eyebrow.

"Well, at least you're admitting he was your boyfriend now," she said. "That's a start."

James would have agreed if he didn't think it was too little too late. What did it matter if he admitted it or not? Matt wasn't around to hear it. He was gone and he wasn't coming back.

* * * *

James had been rushed off his feet all day. He'd just made himself a cup of coffee when the bell over the door chimed and in walked Betty McCormick and her sister May. Their appearance surprised him even more than Brittany and Jane's had the week before. Betty had made her feelings about James' sexuality clear at the funeral and, as the sisters were pretty much thick as thieves, he hadn't expected to see either of them again — except maybe at neighbourhood watch meetings, which he'd been avoiding.

When he'd been seeing Matt, James had worked himself up so much about what people thought about him, he'd envisaged receiving a cold shoulder from practically the entire town. It was stupid, and he knew he'd let his imagination run riot, but he hadn't been able to rein it in. But in the weeks since Matt had left, he'd learnt that actually no one in the town seemed to know about his sexuality. So Betty had obviously been keeping the information to herself, which was the biggest surprise of all. Usually she loved to gossip.

James had been making a point of telling everyone he spoke to that he was gay, just slipping it casually into the conversation whenever he got the chance. He'd reasoned with himself that it was better for people to find out the truth from him than hear it from the town gossips. That way he could gauge people's reactions when they found out, and mostly they'd been good. He didn't know what he'd expected exactly, but it hadn't been that. But the main reason he'd been telling people was because he thought, if he could get used to saying and hearing it, he could get used to living with it. He'd found that the more he said it, the easier it became. He didn't want to hide away anymore.

May was smiling brightly as she took her usual booth seat at the back of the diner. Betty had a scowl on her face, but that was nothing new. James took a deep breath and walked to their table.

"Ladies," he greeted. "Lovely to see you again. How have you been keeping?"

"Not too good, actually," May said. "I've been a little under the weather. Ear infection. It knocked me for six, but I'm a lot better now."

"Glad to hear it," James said.

She nodded. "The doctor said that was probably the reason for my dizzy spells recently. That's why we haven't been in. This is my first time out of the house in over two weeks."

"Really? Well, it's good to see you back to your old self." James was surprised to hear that the sisters' absence had had nothing to do with them finding out about his sexuality, although he should have known better. But it did make him feel like an idiot.

Not everything in this world revolves around you, dumbass.

"How is that lovely young man of yours coping with his loss?" May asked. "I haven't seen him since the funeral. Give him our love, won't you?"

"Uh..." *Oh God.* James should have anticipated that question, but he hadn't. The very mention of Matt made his stomach lurch. He had no idea how to respond, but thought it best to be honest. "Actually Matt and I are no longer together," he admitted, trying not to choke on the sorrow those words caused. "Matt went back to Iowa a few weeks ago."

"Oh, I'm sorry to hear that," May said. "I hope you two can work it out. He's such a nice boy."

"A very nice boy," Betty agreed with a nod of her head.

James nearly swallowed his tongue. *No snide remark?* "Yeah, he is," he mumbled. "Uh, what can I get for you ladies?"

"We're not here to eat." Betty straightened her shoulders and pinned James in place with the cold, mean stare he was so used to seeing on her face. "We have a complaint."

When May sighed very dramatically and rolled her eyes at her sister, James couldn't help the chuckle that burst from his chest. Just what in the hell had he been so worried about for all these years? As he stood there listening to Betty complain about his absence in the neighbourhood watch meeting again, he couldn't understand why he'd let things get so out of hand. He'd blown everything up to such tremendous proportions in his mind that he'd been afraid to even walk down the street with Matt for fear of public flogging, and yet no one gave a damn what he did in his personal life, not really. He could see that now.

And he had to ask himself if he really cared what a small minority of people thought. What did a few small-minded people matter in the grand scheme of things? Surely all that mattered was him and Matt. His family were the only people that James really cared what they thought, and they all loved Matt. Just as he did. Just as he always would, but it was too late now, wasn't it? Would it be possible for Matt to forgive him again?

The diner got busier as the day wore on, busier than he'd seen it in weeks, in fact, but James' mood darkened. The weight of what he'd done, of how he'd fucked up everything, pressed down on his chest until he was damn near suffocating from it. James knew without question that Matt could have made him happy for the rest of his life. He thought about how Matt's presence alone made him smile with a joy he'd never experienced before they'd got together. He'd known something was missing in his life, he'd known he was lonely, but he'd never realised just how much of the void Matt had filled until he was gone. He'd missed Matt when they'd parted ways at eighteen, but the way he'd felt then didn't come close to the pain in his chest he was experiencing now. It was debilitating. It weighed him down, sucked him into a chasm of black despair that was unrelenting in its bleakness. He couldn't breathe in this void. And he knew the only way out, the only way to stop suffocating, was to see Matt. Matt had the power to make everything all right again. If only he could find it in his heart to forgive James one last time, James would be everything Matt needed him to be and more. Matt had to forgive him.

* * * *

"Thanks again, sir. I appreciate your time and thank you for calling me personally to let me know. Absolutely, I'm looking forward to it. I'll see you then."

Matt hung up the call and tossed his cell phone onto the sofa before slumping down onto the cushions himself. He leaned his head back, closed his eyes and let out a long sigh. It had taken him three weeks to find a new job, but he'd finally managed it. It had better prospects than his last job and it paid more money. He should have been happy about that, but happiness wasn't an emotion he was capable of right now.

But you know how you can be happy again, don't you? Don't be such a pussy, Matt. Call him. Tell him that you're sorry. Beg him to take you back. It might not be too late. Call him.

But what's the point? Nothing has changed. You can't live like that, always having to hide away from the world, hiding the way you feel.

Yes, I can. I can do it. If it means I'll get to be with James, I'll do it gladly.

The inner debate Matt had been having with himself since

the night he'd walked out of the restaurant raged on, driving him damn near insane. His heart was already grieving his father and the ache from losing James as well just wouldn't go away. It was a constant reminder of what he'd done. He hated himself for having walked out on James, but at the time James' reaction to him had felt like the last straw. The look he'd seen in James' eyes as he'd snatched his hand back had been like a knife to Matt's already damaged heart. But the more he came to think about it, the more he thought he'd made the biggest mistake of his life by walking away.

Matt was sure James cared for him, and he knew it had to be hard for someone who had been in the closet his entire life to suddenly lead an openly gay lifestyle. He should have been more lenient. He should have cut James some slack, just like he'd asked. Maybe James had needed more time to get used to the idea of them being together. Why couldn't he have given him that? What would a little time have cost him? But it was pointless thinking on what might have been. Maybe James hadn't cared about him as much as Matt had thought. After all, it had been over three weeks since they'd last seen one another and James hadn't called, had he? He hadn't made the slightest attempt to get in touch and his silence spoke volumes.

The loud chime of Matt's doorbell yanked him from his thoughts and he stared in the general direction with an overwhelming sense of resignation.

He took a deep and somewhat calming breath. "Better get this over with," he murmured.

Rising from the sofa, he walked out into the hall until he was at the front door, eyeing it warily. When it rang a second time, he nearly jumped out of his damn skin. He braced himself then pulled open the door and stared at his not so welcome guest.

"Hello, Tom," he greeted. "Come in."

As always, Tom looked like a million bucks. His suit was crisp and ironed to within an inch of its life and his silky dark hair was immaculately groomed. He was wearing his usual confident and cheeky grin. It was the grin that had attracted Matt in the first place, but now it made him look arrogant and smarmy. Maybe he'd always looked that way, but Matt had just never realised it before. Maybe he noticed now because he was comparing him to James, who couldn't look arrogant or smarmy if he tried. But Matt didn't want to think about James right now, he couldn't. He wanted to know what the hell Tom wanted and why he'd called, insisting they meet. Tom had told him it was important. Matt doubted that very much, but he'd give him the benefit of the doubt.

"Hey, gorgeous, I missed you." Tom's hand landed on Matt's hip and squeezed then he planted a kiss on Matt's cheek before he pushed past and strode into the house.

Matt flinched then clenched his hands into fists and swallowed down a snarky retort. "What are you doing here, Tom?" He shut the door and followed his ex into the living room. "What is it you want?"

Tom puckered his lips into a pout. "What, no kiss? Didn't you miss me? I haven't seen you for months."

Matt rolled his eyes. "It's been six weeks."

Tom shrugged. "Where have you been anyway?"

"I was home in Missouri. My father died."

"Oh. Sorry to hear that. Why didn't you call me? I could have helped, I would have…"

"You broke up with me!" Matt fumed. "You left me for a woman, remember?"

Tom averted his gaze. "Yeah, about that. I was hasty. I think I might have made a mistake."

"You *think* you might have made a mistake?" Matt snorted. "You are fucking unbelievable!"

"Aww, baby. Don't be angry at me. We all make mistakes."

"Don't 'baby' me. What happened? She see through your bullshit already? Maybe she realised you only wanted to marry her for her money and connections. What?"

"It wasn't like that." Tom scowled. "I liked her, we got along."

"You got along," Matt repeated. "Well, that's great then. Did you tell her that? Because I could be wrong, but I assumed people actually liked it if you were in love with them before you proposed."

"The wedding was her idea!" he ranted.

"So, what happened?"

Tom mumbled out his reply. He spoke so quietly that Matt had to take a step closer and ask him to repeat what he had said.

"I said she caught me with a man." Tom rubbed the back of his neck nervously, avoiding Matt's gaze.

Matt's mouth fell open in shock. "Excuse me?"

"But it wasn't anything serious, baby. It was just sex."

"You were cheating on her? With a man? Just like you were cheating on me with her, you mean? Or were you seeing all three of us at the same time, hmm? Were there more?"

Tom shuffled from foot to foot and remained quiet. He still wouldn't look Matt in the eye.

"Jesus Christ, you sure do like to 'share the love'. How could I not have known about this?"

Tom shrugged. "Come on. It's not like we were serious. We made no commitment to one another. We never said we were going to be monogamous."

Matt shook his head. "That'll teach me not to assume, I suppose. Thank God we were careful."

"I was always careful!" Tom attested. "And none of them meant anything, baby. I won't see any of them again when we get back together."

Matt just stared at Tom incredulously. He couldn't believe what he was hearing. Did Tom honestly believe for one second they were going to rekindle their relationship? *What a dick!* Matt could feel the hysterics bubble up in his chest and he couldn't hold it in. He threw his head back and laughed until his stomach ached and his shoulders shook and tears poured from his eyes. When the laughter finally died down to a giggle, Tom was looking at him like he was all kinds of crazy. He wasn't far off the mark. Matt certainly felt like he was losing his mind.

"What's so funny?" Tom asked at last.

"You honestly believe I'd get back with you? What sort of weak, pathetic, sorry excuse for a man do you take me for?"

"I don't think of you like that. You're strong. Stronger than I ever was."

"That isn't saying much."

"We were good together," Tom whined. "It can be good again. We can make a go of it, build a life together."

Matt hated to admit that he had liked Tom once. There was a time he would have given anything to hear Tom say he wanted them to become more serious, to build something permanent and to carve out a life together. But being with James had taught Matt he couldn't settle for less than exactly what he wanted. And what he wanted was to be loved, *truly* loved, and to be respected. He wanted his partner to be proud to walk down the street with him, not to flinch when he touched him. Was that too much to ask? *Isn't that what most people want?*

Tom strode across the room and grabbed Matt around the shoulders. "Think about it, will you? You and I are not so different. Neither of us wants to be alone. Well, we don't have to be. Not anymore—we have each other."

Even though he knew what a really stupid idea that was, there was a part of Matt that wanted to grab the offer with both hands and not let go.

Chapter Ten

James glanced at the speedometer and squeezed his foot on the accelerator. Now that he'd made the decision to see Matt, he couldn't get to Iowa quick enough. His stomach felt like a hive of nervous activity and his mind was flitting between the precious images of Matt he'd been saving up. Matt sitting on the sofa in Maria's house, laughing at something Hope had said. Matt naked by the river, the sun casting a warm glow over his smooth, olive-toned skin. Matt lying on his bed, his body bathed in sweat and his head thrown back in ecstasy as he shouted out James' name. Every image was crystal clear in his mind's eye, as though Matt were sitting right next to him. When he concentrated hard enough he could smell him, too — taste him even.

"I miss you," James breathed, the whispered words getting swallowed by the hum of the engine as the car roared along the highway.

I miss you more than I ever thought possible. Please don't tell me it's too late. It can't be too late.

It had already started to get dark by the time James pulled up outside Matt's house, but he'd driven to it on autopilot, remembering the way as though he made the journey every single day. This was the third time he'd sat in his car outside Matt's house, but he'd never been inside, never even walked down the narrow path past the neatly manicured lawn and stood outside Matt's front door. It was ironic that, just like the two previous times he'd been here, James had come to apologise, but this was the first time he'd felt as though his whole life were riding on Matt's decision to forgive him or not.

He had the steering wheel in an iron-tight grasp while he psyched himself up to get out of the car and do what he'd just driven over six hours for. But while he chastised himself for being an idiot, a man whose face he vaguely remembered passed by his car and strolled up the path to Matt's front door. James' breath caught in his throat and his stomach knotted as he watched and waited. Was that Matt's ex-boyfriend? The man pressed the doorbell and a moment later the door opened and Matt's beautiful face appeared. James could feel the bile rising in his throat as the man kissed Matt on the cheek, his hand intimately touching Matt's hip as he passed and made his way into the house. Matt closed the door behind them, and James had to roll down the car window so he could suck in a breath. It didn't help. His heart hammered in his chest as he fought off a wave of sickness.

He was too late. James had left it too damn late. Matt had very clearly moved on, or back, as the case may be. He'd got back together with his ex. James could feel his heart shattering into a thousand little pieces all over again and he was taken back to the night Matt had walked out on him in the restaurant. He should have done something then, he should have run after Matt and got down on his knees and begged Matt to forgive him and to give him another chance, but he hadn't. He'd waited until he'd come to the realisation that he didn't want to live without Matt, but he'd waited too long. Matt didn't want him anymore.

Eyes closed, he rested his head against the steering wheel while he breathed in slowly through his nose and out through his mouth. A part of him wanted to be angry with Matt for moving on so quickly. How could he be with someone else already? Hadn't James meant anything to him? But he really couldn't blame Matt. Maybe this man gave him what he needed. Maybe he treated him better and didn't snatch his hand away when Matt tried to touch him, as though Matt had some disease he was afraid to catch.

James put the car in drive and pulled away from the

sidewalk. He couldn't believe it was too late, that he wouldn't be able to share the rest of his life with Matt, never get to wake up next to him again or feel butterflies dance in his stomach when Matt smiled at him. How had it come to this? James felt raw, exhausted. He had to fight so damn hard to stop the tears that were building behind his eyes from falling. Why did he have to screw up everything?

As he drove back out towards the highway, the voice in James' head was screaming at him to turn the car around and knock on Matt's damn door. He wanted Matt to say it was over to his face so he could see the truth of it in Matt's eyes. How could it be real until Matt had spoken the words out loud?

But what about his ex? Isn't his presence proof enough that it's over?

Don't be such a coward, go back there and make him tell you to your face. You'll never rest easy until you hear him say the words.

Mind made up, James did a U-turn in the middle of the road. He never listened to the damn voice in his head, but this time it seemed like the right thing to do. If it really was over between the two of them, then so be it, but James needed to hear the words from Matt's mouth before he could really believe them. Nothing less would do. Within minutes he had parked the car outside Matt's house and was striding down the path.

* * * *

"So what you're saying is you'd settle for me rather than have to be on your own, is that it?"

Tom averted his gaze. When he finally turned his head and met Matt's eye, he was frowning. "What do you want me to say, Matt? What the hell do you want—fireworks?"

Tom's words smarted. What was wrong with wanting something special? Isn't that what everyone wanted from their relationship? Matt straightened his shoulders and scowled at Tom. "Yes, damn it, I want fireworks. I wouldn't settle for someone and I'd expect the same in return. I want someone that loves me with every fibre of their being, not someone that's merely making do."

Tom snorted. "You've been watching too many movies. It isn't like that in real life. Not for men like us. I know your father was your last living relative. Wouldn't you rather be with me than be on your own?"

"Who said it's either or? Don't be so arrogant as to presume I'd be on my own, Tom."

Tom's smarmy grin got wider. "You might find someone, but let's be honest here. He wouldn't be me, would he?"

Thank God for that.

The doorbell sounded before Matt had the chance to reply, which was a good thing for Tom because the insult had been on the tip of Matt's tongue.

"You expecting someone?"

"No, but whoever it is, their timing couldn't be more perfect. Tom, you said what you came here to say and I've heard more than enough. There is no way in hell I'm going to get back with you. Not now, not ever. I'd like you to leave."

"What?"

"You heard me. I want you to go."

Matt walked out into the hall, hoping that Tom would be behind him. When he looked over his shoulder and Tom was nowhere in sight, he rolled his eyes and opened the front door. His breath left him in a whoosh when he locked eyes with James, who was standing on his doorstep, looking like a dog that had just been scolded. Matt couldn't speak. His mouth was devoid of all moisture and every muscle in his body felt tense. He could do nothing but stare at the face of the man who had touched his heart like no other ever could. He knew that as surely as he knew his own name.

When he finally found his voice he asked, "What are you doing here?" The words were not what he'd meant to say at all, but they were already out of his mouth.

"I... I'd like to talk to you. I know I don't have any right to make requests, but… Can I come in?"

Matt nodded and stepped aside then remembered that Tom was still in the living room and he hesitated. "Uh, can you give me a minute?" He looked over his shoulder and sighed.

"If you have company, I can come back or…"

"No," Matt said quickly. Now that James was standing in front of him, he never wanted to let him out of his sight again. "This will only take a minute."

James stared into Matt's eyes for a long moment. Matt wasn't sure what he saw there but it must have been enough to reassure him because he nodded, the corners of his mouth curving up ever so slightly. "Of course."

He left James standing by the door and went back into the living room to face Tom. When Matt entered, Tom was standing near the window, his hands clasped behind his back. He turned to meet Matt's eye and scowled.

"I asked you to leave, Tom, and I wasn't joking."

"What's the rush, huh? You don't want your new boyfriend to hear something he shouldn't?" Tom spat out the words and crossed the room quickly until he was in front of Matt. "Is that was this is about? Are you fucking someone else?"

Matt felt his anger start to rise. "What the hell has it got to do with you? You left *me*, if I remember correctly, for a woman you'd been seeing when we were together. Or did you conveniently forget that part…again? And from what I've just learned, she wasn't the only one. So why the hell should I feel guilty for seeing someone after we split up?"

Tom let out a deep sigh and avoided his eye. "I said I was sorry."

"Actually, you didn't."

Tom opened his mouth but no words came out. It didn't matter. Matt had heard enough. More than enough.

"Tom, look it doesn't matter anymore. It's over between us."

"I just want you to give me another chance, that's it."

168

"I'm sorry. I can't do that. You had plenty of chances. You obviously didn't want a relationship with me or you wouldn't have left. You wanted to play the field. It's not my problem if you found out too late that that isn't what you wanted after all. It's too late for us to try again. I moved on and you need to do the same."

Tom's eyes grew dark with anger. "Is this because of him?" he asked, his gaze shifting to the doorway.

"No. This has nothing to do with James."

"Don't fucking lie to me!" Tom grabbed hold of Matt's arms and squeezed hard enough to leave a bruise.

"Tom! Get off me!" Matt shouted.

"If you don't get your hands off him in the next five seconds, I swear to God it will be the last thing you ever do," James said, striding into the room until he stood next to them. His beautiful blue eyes were dark with fury.

Tom looked from James to Matt and back again before letting go of Matt's arms. "You'll regret this," he spat.

"Just get out of here, Tom."

With a final glare, Tom marched out of the room. A moment later Matt heard the front door slam then he turned to meet James' eye.

"I didn't need your help." Matt rubbed his hands up and down his arms to soothe the sting left behind from Tom's fingers. "I could have handled him on my own. I'm not some small, defenceless female you need to protect, you know. If that's how you see me, you can—"

"It's not! I don't see you that way at all! Jesus, I was only trying to help."

Matt had spent a lot of time thinking about what it would be like to see James again and what he would say to him. In none of his imaginings had they ended up fighting. He suddenly felt like shit. James had driven a long way to see him and Matt was acting like an ass. He took a deep breath and hoped his apology would be enough.

"I'm sorry. I shouldn't have gone off on you like that. I know you didn't mean anything by it. What are you doing here anyway?"

James looked surprised by the question. He looked around the room as though the answer was hiding on the bookshelves or in one of the paintings on the wall. He rubbed the back of his neck while he chewed on his bottom lip. "I, uh... Crap—this is harder than I thought it would be. And I had this big speech planned and..."

"You had a speech planned?"

James nodded. "Spent the entire journey up here going over it in my head until I got it just right, only now I can't remember a damn word of it." He laughed nervously and massaged his neck again.

"Do you remember the gist of it?"

James nodded. "There was begging. Lots of begging. And grovelling. I know I was supposed to get down on my knees at one stage. I was supposed to tell you that I love you and that I'll always love you and that I know I was an idiot and I know I was scared, but I'm not afraid anymore. I meant to tell you if you'll just give me another chance you'll see that we are made for each other and I'll do my damnedest to prove that to you every single day.

"I also wanted to tell you that I'd be proud and honoured to spend the rest of my life with you at my side, be that in private or in public. And I meant to tell you that I've missed you. Every second you've been gone has felt like an hour and every hour has been like a week. I can't sleep if you're not lying next to me, but in the mornings I don't want to get out of bed. And I wanted to tell you that I'm not me without you." James finally sucked in a deep breath. "I think that was about the gist of it."

Matt took a step closer to James and placed a hand under his chin, his fingers curling around into James' hair. A lump had been forming in his throat throughout James' speech and he couldn't seem to swallow it down to reply. When he finally managed it, his voice was hoarse, like he'd just sucked down a packet full of cigarettes. "As speeches go, it was a pretty good one. But I think getting down on your knees to beg might have been overkill."

"Oh, I wasn't going to get down on my knees to beg. I was going to get down on my knee to do this."

Matt looked on in confusion as James pulled a small black box out of his jeans pocket and, just like he'd said he was going to do, he got down on his knee. He opened the box to reveal a thick silver band.

"Marry me, Matt."

The lump that had taken up residence in Matt's throat got even bigger and, before he could stop them, big, fat tears spilled out of the corners of his eyes. When he opened his mouth to speak, all that came out was a strangled sob and then he fell to his knees, grabbed hold of James' face and kissed him hard.

James didn't know what had happened. One minute he was looking up into Matt's tear-filled eyes, praying the love of his life still loved him back, and the next he was lying on the ground, flat on his back with Matt sprawled on top of him, kissing him passionately and grinding their hips together roughly. James went with it. He dropped the ring box and used both hands to grab hold of Matt's ass and press them closer still. It didn't matter how deep his tongue pushed into Matt's mouth or how close their bodies were, James needed more. He wanted closer and deeper and just…more. Matt gave it to him. He gave him everything, but…

James pulled back to take a breath. "So, this is definitely not a no," he gasped out.

Matt grinned and captured his mouth again, pushing his tongue inside, while he slid his hand between them and fumbled with the button on James' jeans.

"Not a no. 'S a yes," he said into James' mouth. "It's a big, fat, holy hell yes."

James chuckled until Matt planted a kiss on him that was anything but funny. It was hot and sweet and quite possibly the best damn kiss he'd ever known. The noises that were coming out of Matt's mouth were driving him crazy. They were some sort of cross between a moan, a whimper and a growl and they combined to push James closer to the edge. James thought he could resist. He thought he could hang on, but then Matt's fingers slid inside his briefs and wrapped around his cock and he was fighting a losing battle.

James came, hard. His head slammed back onto the rug and every muscle in his body grew taut as he spent himself in Matt's hand. When he stopped shaking and juddering from his release, he looked up into Matt's eyes and saw pure joy shining back at him. Matt's face was flushed. His nostrils were flared and he looked as though he were fighting for breath.

"Lemme suck you."

Matt shook his head. "Want more. Want you inside me when I come. Let's go upstairs."

James had no idea how they made it to the bedroom, he couldn't remember anything except the taste of Matt's lips and the feel of his hand on his now overly sensitive cock. But he'd be damned if the little strokes and caresses weren't starting to make him hard again.

They'd had to stop halfway up the stairs when James managed to get Matt's jeans undone and pulled halfway down his hips. Matt hadn't been wearing any underwear and his swollen cock, moist with pre-cum, was just too hard to resist. Without preamble he slid it into his mouth and swallowed it down to the base. Immediately Matt's hands fisted in his hair, holding him in place while he thrust gently into James' mouth. The feel of Matt's cock — the taste, the solid weight of it sliding over his tongue — was enough to bring James back to full hardness. When Matt started whimpering and thrusting with more zeal, James pulled off, not wanting Matt to come yet.

When they reached Matt's bedroom, they were quick in taking off each other's clothes — too hot, too excited for any slow striptease. Naked, their bodies moist with sweat, they slid together as hands touched each other seemingly everywhere at once. James couldn't get enough of touching Matt. He'd been deprived of it for the past month and he was making up for lost time, relearning every dip and curve, every bone.

Matt's eyes were hooded and full of promise. "God, I need you," he said, desperately gripping James' hips and pulling him closer so that their cocks rubbed together side by side. Matt's voice, like the softest velvet, wrapped around James, caressing and teasing him until he couldn't take any more. He led Matt towards his bed while he kissed him long and hard.

"Where's the stuff, Matt?"

"Huh?"

"Lube, condoms."

"Oh. Uh, in that drawer," he said, pointing to the nightstand farthest from them.

When it didn't look as though Matt was going to move, James climbed over the bed and pulled open the drawer. The lube was right where Matt had said it would be, but he couldn't see any condoms. He rooted around some more.

"Jesus Christ, you have got to be kidding me."

"What is it?"

"Can't find any condoms."

"What?" Matt was around the bed in two seconds flat and peering into the drawer.

"You keep them anywhere else?"

"No." Matt's shoulders slumped and he fell back onto the bed with one arm covering his face. James heard a low moan and he chuckled.

"It's not the end of the world, you know. We can do other stuff."

Matt lowered his arm and peered out from behind it. "When is the last time you got tested?"

As soon as James realised where Matt was going with this line of questioning, he groaned and sat down on the bed next to Matt. His dick definitely liked the idea.

"A couple of months ago—was negative. But you think

this is a good time to be having this conversation?"

Matt sat up and stared into James' eyes. "It's as good a time as any." Suddenly Matt's face was filled with colour. "Mine was right after the first time we had sex," he said quietly. "I hadn't been tested since I first started seeing Tom, and, even though we'd always been careful, I figured I should get it done. Was negative."

"So..." James said.

"Yeah, so..."

"You think we should...?"

Matt shrugged. "We're serious about each other. We're both in this for the long haul. Hell, it was only twenty minutes ago you asked me to marry you and I'm wearing your ring. If we can't trust each other now, when can we?"

"You're... You're wearing my ring?" James grabbed hold of Matt's hand and, sure enough, the engraved silver band sat snugly on Matt's finger. "How?"

Matt's face got even redder. "You were busy. I grabbed it. Wanted to be wearing it when you fucked me."

James smiled so wide his face ached. "I think that's the sweetest thing you've ever said to me." He leant forward and stole a mind-numbing kiss.

"So does that mean we're...?"

"Yeah, it does," James replied. And then he kissed Matt until he could barely breathe, let alone talk.

It only took a few seconds of his body sliding against Matt's before his cock was back to full mast and aching to be buried inside Matt. He shivered. The thought turned him on so damn much. While they kissed and stroked and teased, James grabbed the lube and used it to prepare Matt and himself. In no time Matt was writhing on the bed and bearing down on his fingers. With shaky hands, he applied more slick to himself.

"I've never done this before," he admitted as he lined up, his cock barely skimming the entrance to Matt's body. "Bare, I mean."

Matt was lying on his back, one knee pulled against his

chest, the other resting over James' shoulder. "Then it'll be the first time for both of us. I like that."

"Me too. You ready for me?" When Matt nodded, James pushed forward and after the first point of resistance his cock slid in slowly, inch by agonising inch. Holy hell, it was hot. Better than he'd ever imagined it would feel. Too good, in fact. He nearly came right then and there.

"Christ, Matt—'s good."

When he looked down he realised Matt was having his own problems. His hand was squeezing his dick hard and his eyes were screwed shut.

"You okay?" he asked.

When Matt opened his eyes, they were dark, lust-filled and almost wild in their intensity. "Don't move!" he warned. "Christ, don't move, please."

James didn't move. He barely breathed. The sensation was too damn good and Matt's reaction was turning him on even more. It was difficult to keep still when all he wanted to do was thrust into Matt's tight heat, but he just about managed it.

"Tell me when you're good to go."

Matt was practically vibrating beneath him, his breath coming in short, sharp pants.

"Now…" was all James needed to hear before he let go, thrusting inside with vigour.

He soon set up a rhythm, plunging into Matt as deep as he could go before pulling almost all of the way out and thrusting back inside. A part of him wanted to slow down, to savour the feeling and to make it last, but he knew he didn't have that much control. He grabbed Matt's cock and began to stroke in time with the movement of his hips. Matt went wild beneath him, writhing and bucking up to meet each thrust, his back arched, his head pressed back into the pillow. Matt had his hands on James' ass, his fingers biting into James' skin, encouraging his movements and pulling him closer still.

Matt's dark hair was stuck to his head with sweat and his

face was flushed. James didn't think he'd ever seen a sight as erotic. He leant forward and kissed Matt, pushing his tongue inside while keeping up the strokes of his hand on Matt's cock, his hips moving as if of their own accord.

Each slap of flesh against flesh was met with a cry or a moan or a whimper. The sweet noises Matt made joined with James' own grunts of pleasure and sounded loud to his ears. All of his senses seemed heightened, in fact. Matt's scent surrounded him, bathed him. Matt's touch left a trail of gooseflesh in its wake. Matt's hands fisted in the sheets and when he looked up and met James' gaze, his eyes filled with something like desperation — James lost it.

"Jesus, Matt!" Another couple of thrusts was all it took. He stroked Matt's cock harder and as he came in his ass, buried deep, he felt Matt's cum splash over his hand and coat his stomach.

"James!"

Matt's ass felt like a vice around his cock, pulling him deeper and milking out his release. He didn't want the sensation to ever end, but at the same time it was too much, too intense.

When they both finally stopped shaking, James fell forward, his hands braced on either side of Matt's head. "I love you," he whispered.

The raw emotion he saw in Matt's eyes tugged at his heart. "I know. And you know I love you too. Sometimes I can't believe how much, or how I got this lucky."

* * * *

They dozed for a few hours and when James woke up, Matt's head was resting on the pillow, facing him. His hand was tucked under his chin and he was making the cutest snuffly noises James had ever heard. He never wanted to get up. He wanted to freeze time, to be stuck in this moment forever.

I'm the lucky one, Matt. And I'll never forget it. I promise you

I'll make you happy. I promise I'll make you proud of me.

As soon as Matt opened his eyes and saw James watching him, his mouth curved up into a shy smile. "Hey."

"Hey, yourself. You sleep okay?"

Matt nodded and yawned, stretching out his arms and legs. He laughed. The sound was carefree and like music to James' ears. "Like a log. You?"

"Best sleep I've had in weeks, actually, even though it was brief." He leant forward and kissed Matt, lingering for a moment, tracing the seam of Matt's lips with his tongue. He slipped his hand around Matt's waist and pulled him close until Matt's head was resting against his chest.

"I missed you," he said into Matt's hair. "Can't believe I was so stupid. I nearly lost you."

Matt shook his head. "It wasn't all your fault. I've been doing a lot of thinking since I got back here and I have an apology to make to you, too."

"What for?" James couldn't think of anything Matt would have to be sorry for.

Matt sighed. "I knew this was all new for you. I knew how hard it was. You've hidden that part of yourself your entire life. I should have been more patient, I should have—"

"No," James started to argue, but Matt cut him off.

"It's true, James. I was hurt, but when I calmed down I came to realise that the way you acted was just a gut reaction because you'd been so used to hiding. It wasn't a personal slight against me and I shouldn't have taken it that way. For weeks now I've been planning on going back to Providence and begging your forgiveness. If you hadn't shown up today, I doubt I would have lasted another week before I cracked. Couldn't, I missed you too much."

James didn't know what to say. He couldn't believe Matt felt that way. It made him love the man lying in his arms even more, if that were possible. "I suppose we're going to have to decide what we're going to do about living arrangements."

"Huh?"

"Well, your home is here. It wouldn't be fair of me to ask you to come back to Providence. I guess I could get Angela to run the diner full-time and I could move here. I'm sure I could find a job here."

Matt pulled back and met James' gaze. "You'd do that for me?"

"I'd do anything for you," James said with conviction.

Matt kissed him hard then and didn't pull away until they were both breathless. "I love you for that," he said at last, "but there's no need. Providence is my home, not Des Moines. I've already got a buyer for this house and I just found out earlier that my application was successful for a position just twenty miles outside of Providence. I start work there the week after next. So I have just enough time to pack up here and arrange to get my things shipped home."

James couldn't believe what he was hearing. "Really?" he asked, his voice sounding small and more insecure than he would have liked. "You're coming home?"

Matt's smile was bright and absolutely infectious. It did funny things to James' stomach.

"Of course. How else do you think this marriage thing is going to work?"

Epilogue

Six Months Later

James stuck his head through the door to the kitchen to find his chef. Anthony was standing at the stove, stirring something in a large cast-iron pot. He looked over at James and raised his eyebrow.

"Something I can do for you, boss?"

James grinned. "Yep, you can make another batch of peach pie."

Anthony shook his head. "Aren't folks sick of that yet? You know, I've a mind to take it off the menu. I've got this strawberry and key lime pie I was thinking about swapping it for."

James pretended to look horrified. "Don't you dare! You know very well the peach and pecan is our best seller." James gave a jerk of his head towards the diner. "The terrible twosome just came in. Could you cut me a slice to take to them?"

"Rather you than me." Anthony grinned. "Coming right up."

James nodded his thanks and turned to walk back into the diner. He paused at the last minute. "Oh, and the strawberry and key lime? I'm all over that."

Anthony grinned. "Thought you might say that."

Betty and May were waiting for James in a booth seat near the back. He strolled across the room, in no rush to get to his ear bashing, and took a seat opposite them.

"Anthony's getting that for you," he said to May. "Won't take long. Now, what can I do for you ladies today?"

James held his breath and waited for the words 'We're here to make a complaint' from Betty's lips. They never came.

"Oh, nothing," May said. "We just thought we'd pop in and say hello. Share a slice of your delicious pie."

James cocked his head to the side, his eyebrows scrunched together. He couldn't believe what he was hearing. He was tempted to look around the diner for the hidden cameras. What? No neighbourhood watch meeting he'd missed? No dog mess on the sidewalk outside the diner Betty wanted him to personally clean, even though he didn't own a dog? No earthquake in China he could have prevented? May must have noticed the confusion on his face because she shook her head and chuckled.

"My, my. Are we really that bad?" she asked.

You're not.

"Do we only ever come in if we have something to complain about?"

"Of course not," James replied.

Betty scowled and looked to the kitchen. "That pie is taking a long time, isn't it? What is the chef doing in there, slacking?"

James couldn't hide his grin. There was the Betty he knew and loved. Right on cue, Anthony stuck his head through the hatch. "Pie's up, boss!"

James retrieved the slice of pie and left the sisters to eat it in peace. He was strolling from table to table, filling the salt shakers, when Hope came in dragging an exhausted-looking Maria. Their mom was bringing up the rear.

"Hi!" James greeted, giving his mom a kiss on the cheek. He scooped Hope into his arms and planted a kiss on hers for good measure. She giggled and wiped her face. "Hey, sis, what's up?"

Maria rolled her eyes. "Don't even get me started. You know anyone that wants to buy a five-year-old girl?"

"Maria!" James snorted. "Don't listen to a word she says, pumpkin," he said, tickling Hope and making her squeal.

"How was the mall?"

"Too damn busy," Maria groaned.

"Watch your language in front of Hope," their mom chastised.

Maria lowered her gaze, looking suitably scolded.

"You haven't been doing too much, have you?" James asked his mom. "I hope you were taking regular breaks and sitting down lots."

Gladys rolled her eyes. "Yes, dear. I rested plenty, didn't I, Maria?"

"I worry about you, that's all. I don't want to see you in the hospital again." James couldn't have been happier when his mother had finally admitted defeat and retired from her job at the hospital over four months ago. She never did go back after her heart attack, for which James was thankful. It seems seeing the place from the perspective of a patient had opened her eyes and made her make a few changes in her life.

"Trust me, that's the last thing I want too," she said.

"I was watching her, James," Maria said. "You don't have to worry."

"Where is Uncle Matt?" Hope asked.

Gladys checked her watch. "Yes, isn't he here yet? We were hoping to catch him before we have to leave."

"He should be here any minute," James said. "He was stopping off at the store on his way home from work to get a bottle of wine. We have guests coming for dinner."

"Mr Keller and Rory again?" Maria asked.

James chuckled. "Yes and don't let him hear you call him that. He hates it outside of school."

He and James had been spending quite a bit of time with Chris and Rory and found that they liked their company, a lot. They'd run into each other again the last time they went to the Italian restaurant and had ended up sitting together. They'd had a great night and had made plans to go out again the following weekend. It had become a regular occurrence, one he looked forward to.

Chris was back to teaching in the high school again. James had learnt that his dismissal had had nothing to do with the fact he was gay — that had just been gossip. He'd been let go along with several other teachers because of funding, but when the board had got an influx of cash recently, they'd rehired him.

The bell over the door sounded and, when he turned, James' breath caught in his chest and butterflies danced in his stomach, just as they did every time he set eyes on Matt. He couldn't get enough of looking at him — he'd do it all day long if Matt would let him. Matt's gaze caught his and his face broke out into a stunningly beautiful smile.

"Uncle Matt!" Hope squealed and wriggled in James' arms to be let down. He obliged and, as soon as her feet touched the floor, she ran across the room and dived into Matt's arms. Caught off guard, he stumbled, but soon righted himself.

"Hey, gorgeous. What have you been doing?"

"We went to the mall and Grams bought me a new dress!" Hope exclaimed. "It's pink!"

"Wow! Aren't you lucky?"

Matt crossed the room with Hope in his arms. He leant forward and gave James a peck on the mouth. James very nearly scowled when it ended and Matt pulled back. But there'd be plenty of time for that later. Hope giggled and hid her face.

"Hey, Maria," James greeted. "Gladys, how have you been keeping?"

"Good," she replied. "I still have to take it easy, of course, but I feel like I have a new lease on life since I retired."

Maria leaned in near Matt's ear and mock-whispered, "She's teaching the ladies at the bridge club a thing or two. Think one of the gentlemen there has a bit of a crush on her too."

"Maria!" Gladys reprimanded. Matt chuckled and James joined in when he noticed his mother's cheeks fill with colour.

"Where's John?" Matt asked. "I thought he was playing chauffeur today."

"He is," Maria said. "He had to pick something up from his practice. He'll be back to collect us later."

"Guess what?" Matt asked, his face bursting with excitement.

James grinned. "Is this one of those times where I actually have to guess, or are you just going to tell us?"

Matt rolled his eyes. "I spoke to Laney today and she had some news."

James waited. "And?" he asked when Matt wasn't forthcoming with anything further.

"She's pregnant!"

"No kidding! Wow. Is she gonna make it to the wedding?" James' marriage to Matt was all his sister and mother had talked about for months. He and Matt had agreed they wanted a small ceremony with only their close friends and family, but his sister had taken over the whole thing and they feared it might be getting out of control. Whenever Maria or his mom brought it up, James joked he and Matt were going to elope. They had to go up to Iowa for the ceremony, but it would be worth it.

Matt waved off James' concerns. "The wedding is in a month. Laney will only be four months gone, though the outfit she bought won't fit by then. She didn't sound too happy about that."

James chuckled. "I bet she didn't. Why don't you all take a seat?" he asked. "I'll bring the drinks over."

There were murmurs of agreement from everyone and they all ambled over to a booth near the window.

"Oh! Matt! How fortunate we caught you! We need to talk to you about the neighbourhood watch!" Betty McCormick shouted across the room.

James turned his face away to hide his grin. That was why Betty hadn't said anything to him earlier about the watch meeting, and probably the real reason they'd come in—they'd hoped to see Matt. It seemed he was flavour of the week with them now. He continued to tease Matt about that. Matt met his gaze and let out a weary sigh before going to talk to the sisters. He passed by James on his way over there and leaned in close.

"Don't think I didn't see that grin of yours," he whispered, sliding his hand around James' waist, nice and easy. "You're going to pay for that. Just wait until I get you alone tonight."

James turned his head and stole a quick kiss. "Mmm, I can hardly wait."

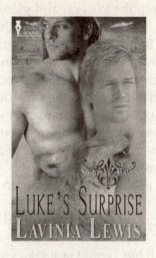

Luke's Surprise

Excerpt

Chapter One

"Luke! Get your butt in here and help me carry these damn boxes!"

Luke put down the book he was reading and rolled his eyes at his brother's hollerin'. He'd been happy to move home after finishing his senior year in college, but his elder brother Kelan had taken to ridin' his ass on a daily basis about anything and everything.

As much as he loved the ranch, he was beginning to wonder if he'd be better off finding himself a place in Houston. Sure he couldn't live for free then like he was now, but the few hundred bucks a month seemed like a small price to pay for his sanity.

"Luke!"

"I'm coming!" Luke shouted back. "Jeez, can't a man have five minutes peace in this place?"

Luke stormed into the kitchen and glared at his brother. Kelan was piling boxes near the door that looked damn near as heavy as he was. Kelan was shirtless, his muscles rippling as he worked and he was sweating up a storm.

At five foot seven and a hundred and forty pounds, Luke was not a large man especially when stood next to Kelan who came up at six foot four. Luke often wondered if they were from the same stock. But looks could be deceiving. Luke's wolf genes meant he was stronger than most men his size. Strength aside, he looked at the boxes and groaned.

Kelan raised an eyebrow and his mouth curled up into a smirk.

"What? Too heavy for you, or you afraid you might break a nail?"

"I might be small but I could still take you." Luke sniffed.

Kelan let out a low, booming roar of laughter.

"I'd like to see the day, little brother. In fact, I'd probably welcome it. Looking out for an entire pack is not all it's cracked up to be, ya know. Some days I'd gladly hand over the responsibility."

Luke was surprised by his brother's response. He knew Kelan loved being alpha of their pack. He'd been born for it. Maybe something had happened that Luke wasn't aware of. That would sure explain why Kelan had been so riled up lately.

"Is everything alright with the pack?" he inquired.

Kelan looked thoughtful for a moment. He opened his mouth to say something then shook his head and picked up a box.

"Nah, it's nothing I can't handle. Now get over here and grab a box, will ya? I need them loaded in the truck."

Luke didn't push. If Kelan wanted to tell him, he'd do so in his own time. His brother could be as stubborn as a mule when he wanted to be. Luke crossed the room and lifted the first box. Yep, they were as heavy as they looked. He grunted and made for the kitchen door.

"What the hell is in these things anyway? Lead?"

"Tools I found in the barn. Used to belong to pop. Figured they were no use to us, so I'm giving them to old man Walker. He just bought another hundred acres and took on two new hands so I reckon he could put 'em to good use."

Luke hid his grin from Kelan as he lugged the box outside. As obstinate as his brother could be, he had a good heart. He was always looking out for members of the pack. It was one of the things that made him such a good alpha.

When they had finished loading the boxes, Kelan went into the house to get cleaned up and grab his shirt. Luke followed him inside. After a quick shower, he caught up with his brother in the kitchen.

"You want me to come with you to Joe's? I can help unload the other end."

Kelan grabbed a bottle of water out of the fridge and took a long gulp before turning to Luke and offering up a mischievous grin.

"You were going to do that anyway. Nice of you to offer though," Kelan chuckled.

"No problem. Anything I can do to help, bro."

Kelan narrowed eyes at his brother's response. Before he could do anything to prevent it, Luke stole the bottle of water out of his hand and drank it down, finishing it quickly. He handed the empty bottle back to Kelan with a snicker.

"You may be bigger than me, but you're as slow as molasses in January."

"That a fact?"

"Yep. I'd say you're...oof!"

Before Luke could finish the sentence, Kelan had tackled him to the floor and had him flat on his back, arms pinned above his head. He straddled Luke's stomach and grinned down at him with a devilish glint in his eye.

"Care to say that again?"

"Sure, you're as slow as...aaarrggh!"

Luke screamed when Kelan began tickling him relentlessly.

"Okay, okay I give." he panted.

"No sir, that ain't good enough. What am I now?"

"You're the biggest, strongest, fastest, brother in the world. Okay?"

More books from
Lavinia Lewis

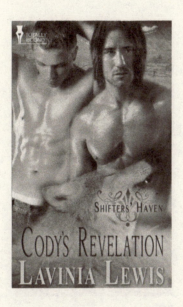

Book two in the Shifter's Haven series

What happens when a werewolf meets his matebut he already belongs to someone else?

More books from

Lavinia Lewis

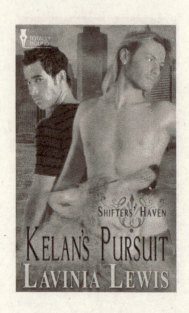

Book three in the Shifter's Haven series

He discovers his life is in danger from an unknown shifter.

About the Author

Lavinia Lewis

Lavinia discovered reading at an early age and could always be found with her nose in a book. She loved getting lost in a fantasy world even then. When her parents bought her a typewriter for Christmas at aged eleven, her fate was sealed. She spent hours dreaming up characters and creating stories. Not a lot has changed. Now when she is not writing you can find her enjoying a new release e-book. Lavinia has lived all over the UK but currently resides in London, England. She has travelled extensively to places including Africa, Asia, Australia, America and most of Europe. Although some of her books are set in Texas she has never visited the state but plans to spend time there in the near future.She is an avid reader and her favourite authors include J L Langley, Carol Lynne, Chris Owen and Andrew Grey. Lavinia particularly loves supernatural fiction and her favourite authors in this genre include Kelly Armstrong, Keri Arthur and Charlaine Harris.Although Lavinia is a huge fan of the romance genre, she will admit to reading anything and everything. She loves horror, a good thriller and if a book has the capacity to make her cry, well, all the better. One thing she does insist on in a book however, regardless of genre is a happy ending, so you will always find one in the books she writes.

Lavinia Lewis loves to hear from readers. You can find contact information, website details and an author profile page at https://www.pride-publishing.com/

PRIDE

PUBLISHING